T0277985

"Ethan Jones plunges us directly in 'human condition.' He recognizes th powerful response to that condition. In a discussion tautly guided by attention to textual specificity and fully informed about current scholarship, Jones invites the reader to be alert to the rich resources of the Psalter. Readers can expect to find in these pages suggestive connections between the imaginative claims of faith and the day-to-day reality of our common life."

—Walter Brueggemann, Columbia Theological Seminary

"In his *Reflections on the Psalms*, C. S. Lewis makes the claim that if the psalms are to be understood and used aright, they must be read as poetry, with an understanding of the distinctive modes of poetry: its tropes and metaphors, its particular way of handling language itself. Jones's excellent book does exactly that, paying scrupulous attention to juxtaposition, paradox, and metaphor and the way these poetic devices work to enhance meaning. As a result, his reading of the psalms is refreshing, prophetic, and strikingly relevant to the age we live in."

—Malcolm Guite, Girton College, Cambridge

"T. S. Eliot once wrote that we are 'distracted from distraction by distraction,' and that was long before our present plethora of mobile devices and social media sites came along. In this thoughtful volume, Jones offers a remedy for the distraction and boredom that plague us—namely, the poetry of the Psalms. What biblical poetry offers us is not relaxation into 'pampered self-care' but 'a better life': one marked by the habits of attention and studiousness. Designed for nonspecialists, this book will prove edifying and instructive for a wide range of readers—from beginners to seasoned experts."

—Brent A. Strawn, Duke University

"Observing that social media can distract us from investing in meaningful relationships, Jones suggests a novel alternative. While the physicality of digital images on our mobile devices provokes curiosity so that we want more, the ethereal quality of poetic images in the book of Psalms provide a reassuring stability. Jones uses several psalms to illustrate their universal poetic appeal in our transient world, offering a fascinating reclamation of ancient biblical poetry for a contemporary setting."

—**Susan Gillingham,** Worcester College, University of Oxford (emeritus)

"*Psalms in an Age of Distraction* is a faith-infused and timely encounter with the Psalms, filled with wisdom for embracing a Scripture-shaped life in the present cultural moment. Fueled by insightful research into distraction, boredom, and attention, Jones's book compellingly presents the poetics of the Psalms as positively soul shaping. Jones illustrates poetry's formational potential before leading the reader through selected psalms, exploring their specific poetic conventions with scholarly insight and making relevant connections for living faithfully in our time."

—**Katie M. Heffelfinger,** Church of Ireland Theological Institute

"Books on the Psalms tend to come in several flavors. Among these are academic studies focused on form, with little to no religious emphasis, and devotional books highlighting the spiritual but ignoring the literary. Jones's book admirably fills the gap by drawing attention to the psalms' poetic features in the service of deepening our understanding and appreciation of the beauty of the Bible's best-known poetic book. With chapters dedicated to individual psalms and their use of various poetic features, Jones unpacks the richness of the psalms rooted in their original language and form."

—**Aaron D. Hornkohl,** University of Cambridge

Psalms in an Age of Distraction

EXPERIENCING THE RESTORATIVE POWER OF BIBLICAL POETRY

ETHAN C. JONES

FOREWORD BY ELIZABETH ROBAR

Baker Academic
a division of Baker Publishing Group
Grand Rapids, Michigan

Published by Baker Academic
a division of Baker Publishing Group
Grand Rapids, Michigan
BakerAcademic.com

Printed in the United States of America

Library of Congress Cataloging-in-Publication Data
Names: Jones, Ethan C., author.
Title: Psalms in an age of distraction : experiencing the restorative power of biblical poetry / Ethan C. Jones.
Description: Grand Rapids, Michigan : Baker Academic, a division of Baker Publishing Group, [2024] | Includes bibliographical references and indexes.
Identifiers: LCCN 2024008545 | ISBN 9781540967640 (paperback) | ISBN 9781540968333 (casebound) | ISBN 9781493447602 (ebook) | ISBN 9781493447619 (pdf)
Subjects: LCSH: Bible. Psalms—Criticism, interpretation, etc. | Poetry—Religious aspects—Christianity. | Distraction (Psychology)—Religious aspects—Christianity. | Attention—Religious aspects—Christianity. | Spiritual formation.
Classification: LCC BS1430.55 J66 2024 | DDC 223/.206—dc23/eng/20240523
LC record available at https://lccn.loc.gov/2024008545

Cover art: *Like Wings*, by Katherine Holmes

Baker Publishing Group publications use paper produced from sustainable forestry practices and postconsumer waste whenever possible.

24   25   26   27   28   29   30   7   6   5   4   3   2   1

— For Emily Rose —

Contents

Foreword

Founder of Psalms: Layer by Layer, Scriptura

It used to be that I liked the idea of the psalms more than I liked the actual psalms themselves. I loved songs based on the book of Psalms because they took a portion and made it into a complete, intelligible experience. Their lyrical expressiveness made my heart swell with longing for the Lord and drew me close to my God.

But taking an individual psalm and understanding it as one complete, intelligible experience was far more difficult. I didn't understand whether the psalmist was pleading in despair or crying out in confidence. I didn't understand how fear could suddenly turn into triumph. Some of the praise in Psalms seemed simplistic and, to be honest, not very powerful. Reading "Praise God!" a dozen times in succession did not move my spirit.

All this changed with the project designated Psalms: Layer by Layer, which has opened my eyes to the psalms as never before. Now, each psalm is an implicit challenge for my soul to join a journey of faith. It is a journey that requires full emotional engagement, full mental engagement, and the engagement of my deepest beliefs, at the very core of my being. A walk of faith is played out before my eyes, through each psalm, and I am asked to walk that same walk, in step with the words of Scripture.

Psalm 118 tells about a near military defeat that will turn into a stunning triumph. The victor cries out that, thanks to the Lord's loyalty, there can never be anything to fear. As I read and pray through Psalm 118, I am challenged to make that my own cry: God is asking me to believe that there can never be anything to fear. He is asking me to be willing to experience near defeats that he will turn into stunning triumphs. When distress arrives, it is as if the psalmist is standing by my side, challenging me: now it will be revealed whether I really believe as he did.

I used to find Psalm 150 boring. How could this be the culmination of the Psalter? Yet now I understand the implicit story: the God of Israel is crowned as king of the universe, and all creation comes to celebrate. Everything, even vocabulary and grammar, becomes oriented to the one goal of praising God as king! One of the most striking features is a poetic device that frames the psalm. Hebrew poetry enjoys playing with the alphabet: one way is to mark a section of poetry as complete by having it begin with *aleph*, the first letter, and end with *tav*, the last letter. Psalm 150 starts with "Praise the Lord! Praise *God* [v. 1, "God" beginning with *aleph*] . . . Praise [v. 6, "praise" beginning with *tav*] the Lord! Praise the Lord!" If we skip the *aleph* to *tav* section, what's left is "Praise the Lord! Praise . . . the Lord! Praise the Lord!" In Hebrew, it's literally "Hallelujah! Hallelujah! Hallelujah!" The poetry is presenting all the content, "from A to Z," as swallowed up in a triple hallelujah.

Every time I explain this poetic feature of Psalm 150, my heart starts to race. The very image of my own life, my own history and all my experiences, from A to Z, one day being swallowed up in praise of our God and king nearly takes my breath away. It hits home, as I realize that praising God is my goal in life.

Traditionally, the mark of a scholar is a dispassionate relationship to the object of study, which is supposed to enable an unbiased approach. But if I were to study the book of Psalms with no emotional engagement, I would miss its very purpose. These psalms are seeking to draw me into a life of faith, into experiencing life more fully and vividly because nothing is left out. Alongside the deepest fears and the greatest joys is the covenant God, who leads me through them all. It is a story of suffering and pain that culminates in riotous joy, in the praise of a victorious king. It is a story about how I am part of a larger story, one that began at creation and will continue until heaven reigns on a new earth. I am invited to play my own role in that story, in which my tears and triumphs become aligned with those of Moses, David, Jesus, and every believer who has prayed or sung the Psalms. The Psalms show me my place in this world and teach me how to live life as a covenant child of God. May the same be true of you.

Acknowledgments

Putting together this book has been a joy from start to finish. It began as a strong yet soft suggestion from my wife. As a scholar, I delight in the technical details of Hebrew and poetry, much of which appears in essays and books for fellow scholars. Emily gently advised me that it was time to put some of my ruminations in print for interested readers who aren't specialists. From that moment, I knew exactly what I needed to write and who I wanted to work with. Anna Gissing at Baker Academic has been my champion, a constant guide, and a steady encourager.

Most of my writing took place in one of my favorite cities in the world, Cambridge, England. Friends, fellow scholars, snow, chapels, and good books meant for a most idyllic winter setting. Once home in the beauty of the Big Easy (New Orleans), I was able to finish the book. I'm immensely grateful to my president at New Orleans Baptist Theological Seminary, Jamie Dew, and my provost, Norris Grubbs, for their support. I'm also thankful for friends and colaborers, especially Charlie Ray and Tyler Wittman, who have sharpened my thinking, writing, and devotion. My research assistant, Sarah Haynes, has been a treasure. Her keen eye, patience, and care have blessed my work.

As will be seen, my view of Psalms has been significantly shaped by Immanuel Community Church in New Orleans. My heart has been habituated by the life of the church, always stimulating and sustaining worship over mere academic theorizing. My pastor, Matthew Delaughter, has been a special gift in this season. I'm forever indebted to George Klein, my mentor and friend, who initially drew me to the well of Psalms. In addition, I must mention Dan Estes, whose encouragement has been constant. Thanks to my dear friend Katherine Holmes for contributing her artwork, *Like Wings*, to the cover. Though she lives across the world, her generous spirit, skill, and faith encourage me in my work.

This book would not be, or not be what it is, without my family. My boys, both lively, sharp, generous, and empathetic, know the psalms by way of song, prayer, and recitation. Their dispositions and knowledge are due mainly to their mother, my wife of wisdom and hospitality, who spurred this project onward and to whom it is dedicated. Lastly, this book is about God, for the book of Psalms is indeed about God—Father, Son, and Holy Spirit. If anything is to be gained in this book, it will be but chaff if it doesn't invite the reader to worship the true and living God.

Abbreviations

General and Bibliographic

AIL	Ancient Israel and Its Literature
ATD	Das Alte Testament Deutsch
BI	Biblical Interpretation
BZAW	Beihefte zur Zeitschrift für die alttestamentliche Wissenschaft
cf.	*confer* (Latin), compare
chap(s).	chapter(s)
EBS	Essentials of Biblical Studies
ed(s).	edition, editor(s), edited by
e.g.	exempli gratia, for example
esp.	especially
ESV	English Standard Version
FAT	Forschungen zum Alten Testament
FC	Fathers of the Church
HThKAT	Herders Theologischer Kommentar zum Alten Testament
JSOT	*Journal for the Study of the Old Testament*
JSOTSup	Journal for the Study of the Old Testament Supplement Series
JTI	*Journal of Theological Interpretation*
JTISup	Journal of Theological Interpretation, Supplements
LHBOTS	The Library of Hebrew Bible / Old Testament Studies
NAC	New American Commentary
NICOT	New International Commentary on the Old Testament
NRSVue	New Revised Standard Version, updated edition (2021)
rev.	revised
SBLDS	Society of Biblical Literature Dissertation Series
SJ	Society of Jesus: Jesuits
trans.	translated by, translator(s), translation
v(v).	verse(s)
ZAW	*Zeitschrift für die alttestamentliche Wissenschaft*

Old Testament

Gen.	Genesis	Eccles.	Ecclesiastes
Exod.	Exodus	Song	Song of Songs
Lev.	Leviticus	Isa.	Isaiah
Num.	Numbers	Jer.	Jeremiah
Deut.	Deuteronomy	Lam.	Lamentations
Josh.	Joshua	Ezek.	Ezekiel
Judg.	Judges	Dan.	Daniel
Ruth	Ruth	Hosea	Hosea
1 Sam.	1 Samuel	Joel	Joel
2 Sam.	2 Samuel	Amos	Amos
1 Kings	1 Kings	Obad.	Obadiah
2 Kings	2 Kings	Jon.	Jonah
1 Chron.	1 Chronicles	Mic.	Micah
2 Chron.	2 Chronicles	Nah.	Nahum
Ezra	Ezra	Hab.	Habakkuk
Neh.	Nehemiah	Zeph.	Zephaniah
Esther	Esther	Hag.	Haggai
Job	Job	Zech.	Zechariah
Ps(s).	Psalm(s)	Mal.	Malachi
Prov.	Proverbs		

New Testament

Matt.	Matthew	1 Tim.	1 Timothy
Mark	Mark	2 Tim.	2 Timothy
Luke	Luke	Titus	Titus
John	John	Philem.	Philemon
Acts	Acts of the Apostles	Heb.	Hebrews
Rom.	Romans	James	James
1 Cor.	1 Corinthians	1 Pet.	1 Peter
2 Cor.	2 Corinthians	2 Pet.	2 Peter
Gal.	Galatians	1 John	1 John
Eph.	Ephesians	2 John	2 John
Phil.	Philippians	3 John	3 John
Col.	Colossians	Jude	Jude
1 Thess.	1 Thessalonians	Rev.	Revelation
2 Thess.	2 Thessalonians		

PART I

Psalms, Poetry, and the Distracted Self

— 1 —

An Age of Distraction

Distraction "is now a universal competency. We're all experts."[1]
We don't need statistics to prove that we're living in a distracted
age. Our lives are the evidence. While talking to friends, they obliga-
torily nod their heads in conversation as they slowly reach for their
phones. They check messages, social media, and more, all while giving
a half-hearted physical cue that they're listening. A car pulls up to a
stoplight, and the driver is thumbing through digital pages at a rapid
rate, hoping to find something interesting. A young married couple
at a restaurant, mildly excited about ordering their favorite dish, sits
scrolling silently, while an elderly couple at an adjacent table does the
same. Finally, a night out without responsibilities, appointments, and
activities, they think. They rest and relax in the comfort of digital
distraction. They return home, tidy the house, and saunter to bed,
all while anticipating a glowing screen of entertainment. These are
normal days for normal people.

This is not a book about digital media—its helps or its harms. This
book is about the book of Psalms. These psalms endure. Throughout
the centuries, Christians have read, prayed, and sung them. Yet the

1. Joshua Rothman, "A New Theory of Distraction," *The New Yorker*, June 16, 2015,
https://www.newyorker.com/culture/cultural-comment/a-new-theory-of-distraction.

daily rhythms of modern life evidence more distractions than biblical texts. My concern has to do with the balance between the two,
but not necessarily in relation to time. Simply putting more Bible
on the daily time sheet and less social media, for instance, is not
what I'm talking about (though it certainly wouldn't be the worst
idea). My interest lies in how both distraction and the psalms can
shape our lives.

There's much more to distraction than we might think at first. Un-
derneath it is something as substantial as it is common: *boredom*. No
doubt we've all been well acquainted with boredom since childhood,
and like distraction, "boredom is a perennial problem."[2] Perhaps
surprisingly, the nature of boredom may in fact be something of a
key to life, for to "understand boredom is to understand oneself."[3]
Boredom can, of course, push in a thousand directions, from reaching for social media to searching for the snooze button, but at its
foundation, boredom "signals a misalignment of our desires with our
environment."[4] Crucially, not all boredom is equal: its consequence
can be serious or silly, leading to anything from a broken marriage
to a group of friends giggling about the latest meme.

In this present age of entertainment, dimly lit faces, and multi-
tasking, *Psalms in an Age of Distraction* makes the positive case for
this biblical book, particularly its significance for the modern moment.[5] Psalms, as a rich collection of poems, remains ready to train
our ears, steady our hearts, teach our prayers, and extend our imagination.[6] The psalms are poetry for the soul, and this poetry shapes us.

---

2. Kevin Hood Gary, *Why Boredom Matters: Education, Leisure, and the Quest
for a Meaningful Life* (Cambridge: Cambridge University Press, 2022), 26.

3. Gary, *Why Boredom Matters*, 9.

4. Gary, *Why Boredom Matters*, 12–13.

5. For a fundamental critique of specific technology relevant to the topic but al-
together too narrow for the chapter at hand, see Tiger C. Roholt, *Distracted from
Meaning: A Philosophy of Smartphones* (London: Bloomsbury Academic, 2023).
See also the thoroughly pointed Jonathan Haidt, "Get Phones Out of Schools Now,"
Atlantic, June 6, 2023. For a practical and thoughtful treatment, see Andy Crouch,
The Life We're Looking For: Reclaiming Relationship in a Technological World (New
York: Convergent, 2022).

6. See, e.g., the recent poems inspired by and in response to the poetry of Psalms:
Malcolm Guite, *David's Crown: Sounding the Psalms* (Norwich, UK: Canterbury,
2021); Michael O'Siadhail, *Testament* (Waco: Baylor University Press, 2022); and

The present chapter sketches out—by way of poets, philosophers, and theologians—what is happening in the interior life on account of our culture of distraction. The purpose here is to shed some light on our context, but not as an exercise in panic, fear, and yearning for some (imagined) past. Instead, taking stock of where we are, we can gather a sense of how poetry in general can cultivate our attention and focus our lives in fruitful ways. More precisely, we want to notice how the poetry does so for the pilgrim who walks with God. In response to the vices that lie in wait for those of us distracted and bored, I present a brief theology of attention to prepare us for how and why reading Psalms is significant for today.[7] Before doing so, however, I introduce the complexity and vexation of the seemingly simple concept of boredom.

Boredom

The novelist David Foster Wallace scratches at what is below the surface of modern society, as he concludes: "Surely something must lie behind not just Muzak in dull or tedious places anymore but now also actual TV in waiting rooms, supermarkets' checkouts, airports' gates, SUVs' backseats. Walkmen, iPods, BlackBerries, cell phones that attach to your head. This terror of silence with nothing diverting to do. I can't think anyone really believes that today's so-called 'information society' is just about information. Everyone knows it's about something else, way down."[8] Wallace's observations lead us to consider the nature of boredom.

The first and most significant category we come to is *existential boredom*. This state speaks to the "disenchantment with life and a struggle to find meaning."[9] A definition or a precise diagnosis of existential boredom is not particularly easy. Among other things,

---

Edward Clarke, *A Book of Psalms* (Brewster, MA: Paraclete, 2020); as well as the pastoral resource by Brent Strawn and Roger van Harn, eds., *Psalms for Preaching and Worship: A Lectionary Commentary* (Grand Rapids: Eerdmans, 2009).

7. See also N. T. Wright, *The Case for the Psalms: Why They Are Essential* (New York: HarperCollins, 2013).

8. David Foster Wallace, *The Pale King: An Unfinished Novel* (New York: Little, Brown, 2011), 93, quoted in Gary, *Why Boredom Matters*, 37.

9. Gary, *Why Boredom Matters*, 21.

it involves muting the vividness of life and imbibing deep disinterest. Someone experiencing existential boredom reads life similar to "the Teacher" in Ecclesiastes: "Everything is vanity" (1:1–2). In a significant way, this bored person is disengaged; yet there can even be a "subtle arrogance" that existential boredom entails.[10] This arrogance illustrates agency in scanning the world and finding nothing of interest or meaning, nothing significant enough for their time, and no idea that offers up enough interest to pique their curiosity.[11]

The second category is *situational boredom*. This boredom, as one would expect, is largely, if not exclusively, based on external conditions.[12] Think of standing in line at the grocery store or waiting at a gate in the airport. We find ourselves in these kinds of unavoidable moments, no matter who we are or what we do as a vocation. Unfortunately, the inescapabilty of situational boredom can intersect with the much more serious existential version noted above. For instance, our "avoidance of situational boredom *intensifies* existential boredom."[13] That is, our common reflex for dealing with dull moments has a troubling effect on our person. This is a significant point that merits reflection.

Imagine, for example, a week when every night closes out with hours of flickering screens. Scrolling on a phone and simultaneously watching shows helps to have some "me time," we say. Weeks add up, months accumulate, and the steady accretion weighs us down. At some point, driving to work or perhaps cutting the grass, we ask ourselves, "What am I doing with my life?" A fog of meaninglessness prevents clear vision. It's as if the only reason we wake up and work is to have incandescent moments of streaming entertainment at night. We intuitively know this isn't right, yet our habits don't align. We know the joy of raising children or the commendation of a life well lived has nothing to do with reveling in boredom and distraction.[14] Even so, for many of us, our lives and aims are disoriented.[15]

10. Gary, *Why Boredom Matters*, 35.
11. Gary, *Why Boredom Matters*, 35.
12. Gary, *Why Boredom Matters*, 21.
13. Gary, *Why Boredom Matters*, 21 (emphasis added).
14. See the cogent David Brooks, *The Road to Character* (New York: Random House, 2015).
15. As Augustine observes, "Living a just and holy life requires one to be capable of an objective and impartial evaluation of things; to love things . . . in the right order, so

It is important to recognize that existential boredom is not sourced primarily from personality: it "rather is a constitutive part of the human condition."[16] In other words, every one of us has to square off with this reality. As above, situational boredom can kindle existential boredom, but it shouldn't be missed that the everyday, mundane nature of situational boredom is set ablaze by the "weariness of satiety." The weighty phrase "weariness of satiety" comes from Robert Louis Stevenson and speaks to the fact that our environment is *not* neutral, but rather overstimulates.[17] Notably, Stevenson's observation came in the year 1880, and obviously much has changed since then: the tools for stimulation are now beyond number. We live in an economy of overstimulation.

Despite the flood of distraction technologies, we need to be clear on the logic here. We're not necessarily distracted or bored *because* of technology, but our propensity to amuse ourselves *with* technology today is nevertheless unmistakable.[18] Technology isn't able to stand in as *the* enemy or *the* problem; yet "there is an extensive leisure industry [e.g., theme parks and streaming shows] that co-opts and gives *shape and direction* to how we envision what leisure is and what motivates us."[19] This shaping effect is precisely what *Psalms in an Age of Distraction* is all about. Motivation and telos meet in the modern ideal of the pampered self that seeks to *turn off* and relax, as on a luxury cruise or in a fully accommodated resort. The book of Psalms is counter to this standard mode of operation. This, of course, is not to say that a cruise or resort is somehow inherently wrong, but I hope it becomes clear that *how* we strive and grope for these moments of *turning off* says much about our view of God as well as our life with him.[20] The psalms will teach us, sometimes gently, other times less so,

---

that you do not love what is not to be loved, or fail to love what is to be loved, or have a greater love for what should be loved less, or an equal love for things that should be loved less or more, or a lesser or greater love for things that should be loved equally." *De doctrina Christiana*, trans. Edmund Hill (Hyde Park, NY: New City, 2007), 1.27.

16. Gary, *Why Boredom Matters*, 66.

17. Gary, *Why Boredom Matters*, 28.

18. Gary, *Why Boredom Matters*, 32.

19. Gary, *Why Boredom Matters*, 67 (emphasis added).

20. Lest we push some of the above descriptions off on those who might earn more money, Gary levels the playing field: "Most of us, given social commitments,

that the aim of life, whether we're in our 20s or 60s, is not to relax into pampered self-care; the psalms envision a better life.

Focal Practice

Over the centuries, wise minds have considered how to combat or reconfigure boredom in order to have a flourishing life. One persistent suggestion has been to choose *focal practices*.[21] These customs serve as a "hearth" of attention: they can shift our vision and change our lives.[22] There is debate among philosophers as to what exactly constitutes a focal practice, but the scope is not my concern.[23] More important is the fact that these practices can be made of the mundane fabric of society.[24] Think of things like gardening, running, playing music, or cooking. At their core, these practices are grounding and have the ability to help us grow and mature. The purpose, however, is not to become an expert or a professional.

At odds with any focal practice is the prevalence of convenience, especially given the prominence of distraction technology.[25] Nonetheless, we should relish the fact that "focal practices, and the things they direct us to carefully engage with, stand in direct opposition to" the frenetic, impatient, overly distracted lifestyle many of us are

and the relentless saturation of amusement, have to participate, to some degree, in cruise-like activities" (*Why Boredom Matters*, 69). A recent example is the fact that in nearly every demographic imaginable, folks will be seen scrolling and tapping their (reasonably expensive) phones while waiting to catch a plane. This is made all the clearer when children as young as one year old have their own tablet to pass their time while traveling. An odd amount of luxury crops up in various sectors of society. These modern forms of leisure may be appropriately interpreted as "self-anesthetization," and this (often unperceived) purpose of leisure pervades modern culture.

21. Notably poetry and acedia meet head-on in the complex and triumphant poetry of T. S. Eliot, as Susan Colón notes: "Eliot rendered in his Christian poetry a characteristically paradoxical way to imagine and appropriate remedies for the acedia that bound so many of his contemporaries in distraction and despair." "This Twittering World," *Religion and Literature* 43 (2011): 86.

22. See Albert Borgman, *Technology and the Character of Contemporary Life: A Philosophical Inquiry* (Chicago: University of Chicago Press, 1987).

23. Cf. Alasdair MacIntyre, *After Virtue: A Study in Moral Theory*, 3rd ed. (Notre Dame, IN: University of Notre Dame Press, 2022).

24. Gary, *Why Boredom Matters*, 93.

25. Gary, *Why Boredom Matters*, 94.

prone to have.[26] A key way by which someone cultivates a flourish-ing life with these practices is to foster a spirit of *study*.[27] This is by no means a novel argument: two of the key figures regularly drawn upon are Thomas Aquinas and Augustine of Hippo. What's more, we need to be clear that study extends well beyond the classroom and that the spirit of study "should pervade every activity," from writing to gardening.[28]

On the overlap of study and focal practice, I think of my wife, whose skill and steady attention to gardening have grown signifi-cantly over the years. Were you to walk into our backyard, you'd enter through a trellised canopy of wisteria, turn to a patch of strawberries, and look over to a satsuma tree adjacent to rows of long beans and okra—all dotted throughout with tall, florescent zinnias. Walking through our kitchen on a given day, you'd see a spread of books and folders, bins of intensely organized seed packets, and an impressively coded Excel spreadsheet. Without ever naming it as such, Emily has been doing a focal practice. This practice removes her from inane distraction and directs her attention to a good work that benefits herself, our family, our neighbors, and our church. Her constant study of gardening has led to an entire cabinet of used jars that sit at the ready for freshly cut flowers to be given at Emily's wish to an unsuspecting neighbor or friend. Smiles and hugs abound through the simple cutting and sharing of homegrown flowers. This activity is a good that necessitates attention.

Like gardening, I argue that reading poetry is one activity that can serve as a focal practice. By this, I mean poetry in general. Attending to the language of poetry calls for care and attention to its sound, movement, images, and more. Elaine James makes use of the image of a labyrinth as she helps readers grasp that walking around within a poem is never pointless: there are "no wrong turns."[29] The primary way to engage poetry, she argues, is to recognize that "the poem

26. Gary, *Why Boredom Matters*, 95.

27. Gary, *Why Boredom Matters*, 95–96.

28. Gary, *Why Boredom Matters*, 101. Later, I sharpen his point with a theological account. For now, I'd simply like to make his argument more specific.

29. Elaine James, *An Invitation to Biblical Poetry*, EBS (New York: Oxford University Press, 2021), 15.

presents questions for us: Will you give your *time* and *attention?*[30]
What's more, she makes clear that "a poem has no shortcut. It asks
its audience to invest time, energy, care, and above all, *attention.*"[31]
It is likely a surprise to no one that it takes time to grow in the skill
of reading poetry.

In my experience, many bemoan poetic literature because they
don't know how it works. While such uninclined readers could use all
kinds of instruction on the technical features of poetry, at the outset
I find it more important to assert that poetry as a form prompts the
spirit of study and wonder.[32] Yet the weight of my argument leads
me to ask, *How much more so for the book of Psalms?* To be sure,
my argument throughout this book is not that reading the psalms is
completely analogous to gardening, running, playing music, or cooking, as if it were just one more practice to select. Rather, I contend
that the poetry of Psalms is meant to capture both the attention and
the imagination of every level of reader so as to lead us in *prayer
and worship of the living God.*[33] The book of Psalms comes to us as
poetry; as such, I find that the form is especially suited to draw us in
and focus our attention on who God is and how we commune with
him in prayer and praise.

Placide Deseille fittingly observes that "one of the most cherished
spiritual practices of the ancient monks was unceasing rumination
upon Scriptural texts, especially the Psalms."[34] The act of reading
psalms helps us to live our way into a new way of living. Poetry
in general is said to be for contemplation, and psalms poetry in

30. James, *Invitation to Biblical Poetry*, 15 (emphasis added).
31. James, *Invitation to Biblical Poetry*, 15 (emphasis added).
32. See, e.g., Jean-Pierre Sonnet, "He Who Makes Wonders: God's *Mirabilia*
in the Hebrew Bible—Between Narrative and Poetry," in *Astonishment: Essays on
Wonder for Piero Boitani*, ed. Emilia di Rocco (Rome: Edizioni di Storia e Lettera-
tura, 2019), 38–39; Luis Alonso Schökel, *A Manual of Hebrew Poetics*, trans. Adrian
Graffy, Subsidia Biblica 11 (Rome: Editrice Pontificio Istituto Biblico, 1988); William
Brown, *Seeing the Psalms: A Theology of Metaphor* (Louisville: Westminster John
Knox, 2002).
33. For an important treatment on prayer in the Old Testament, see Samuel E.
Balentine, *Prayer in the Hebrew Bible: The Drama of Divine-Human Dialogue*, Over-
tures to Biblical Theology (Minneapolis: Fortress, 1993).
34. Placide Deseille, "Acedia according to the Monastic Tradition," *Cistercian
Studies Quarterly* 37 (2002): 297.

particular can serve as a focal practice.[35] For practice to be *focal*, it must reckon with the reality of attention, a topic to which we now turn.

Reading and Attention

Literary critic Alan Jacobs writes on technology, the soul, and attention in an arresting way. In one of his "theses for disputation," he opens with a quotation from philosopher and poet Simone Weil: "There is something in our soul that loathes true attention much more violently than flesh loathes fatigue. That something is much closer to evil than flesh is. That is why, every time we truly give our attention, we destroy some evil in ourselves. If one pays attention with this intention, fifteen minutes of attention is worth a lot of good works." Jacobs highlights agency here in startling terms. He comments on Weil that "genuinely to attend is to give of oneself with intent; it is to say: For as long as I contemplate this person, or this experience, or even this thing, I grant it a degree of dominion over me. But I will choose where my attention goes; it is in my power to grant or withhold."[36] This thesis underscores the costly reality of our attention; it is fair to say that most of us give little thought to this truth. In bingeing on a show or scrolling for hours, we haven't really taken account of how we're giving ourselves to a digital device and its entertainment: we're merely passing the time, we tell ourselves. I say this not to somehow begin loading laws upon us and burying us with guilt. On the contrary, I simply want to consider a more beautiful way to live than mindlessly engaging in these distraction technologies for hours on end.

Jacobs muses on a couple of common phrases regarding attention and provides some philosophical exegesis. For instance, "I wish I had *paid* more attention"; "It needs all the attention you can *give* it." He

35. For the struggle to locate contemplation in relation to the rhetoric of poetry, see Irene P. Garrison, *Persuasion, Rhetoric, and Roman Poetry* (Cambridge: Cambridge University Press, 2019), 9–45, esp. 9–12.

36. Alan Jacobs, "Attending to Technology: Theses for Disputation," *The New Atlantis* 48 (Winter 2016): 17. See also Jacobs, *The Pleasure of Reading in an Age of Distraction* (New York: Oxford University Press, 2011).

responds that "both verbs are necessary." The former once again draws out the cost value, whereas the latter stresses "our freedom of choice." He extends the point and claims, the "planet deserves attention." Fleshing out this truth, he finds that the "beauty of water is something like the opposite of two foul sinners cursing each other: it would be base *not* to be interested in it."[37] The world abounds in matters worthy of attention.

Attending to one thing, wholly and seriously, means not to attend to something else. I simply can't scroll through my phone, watch a football game, and talk with my son about his day all at the same time and equally well. Attempts can be (and have been) made. Nevertheless, I know that I can only do one thing, and that choice matters. When a coworker is struggling with something, even if minor, and I have a lecture to give or a chapter to write or papers to grade, the cost is clear. I have to decide what gets my attention. In any case, the decision has a price: as Jacobs writes, "No moment comes to us twice." Such a realization can sober us to the stark reality of life or stun us into paralysis and inaction. At our best, however, we can take stock of what life is and in turn live well in the moment.[38]

Curiosity and Study

We're often taught and in turn teach that curiosity is a good thing. Summoning schoolchildren to become curious is a fairly normal occurrence. Recently, a fellow professor was praised in print for how curious she is. This is common language for describing something commendable. In the way most of us use the word, curiosity leads to an openness to new things and new information, often coinciding with effort to attain that knowledge. This is all well enough, but when we consider curiosity from a theological point of view, it's surprisingly destructive—and not simply because we can be curious about the wrong things.

37. Jacobs, "Attending to Technology," 18 (emphasis original).
38. See also Alan Jacobs, "Habits of Mind in an Age of Distraction: Small Steps to Meet the Challenge of Hearing God in a Technologically Disruptive Environment," *Comment*, June 1, 2016, https://comment.org/habits-of-mind-in-an-age-of -distraction.

Concerning the search for novelty, Zena Hitz wisely observes that we "fall into the pursuit of spectacles, whether the spectacles of our own actions or the spectacles available to us from the view of the easy chair."[39] This could hardly be more descriptive of our in-between times. Whether the silliness of pop-culture magazines at the grocery checkout or the mind-numbing scroll through social media with so-named influencers, the "spectacle" is a timely value. Study, on the other hand, is a disciplined appetite for knowledge.[40] Drinking in every news line, with endless commentary from talking heads, would miss the mark. The googling of every little, often meaningless, fact hardly defines an orderly life. Information does not by necessity fructify.

Vain and quick scouring of information speaks of an inability to stay focused for any significant amount of time. This is how many of us behave, and we'd likely concede that we need help in this area. At base level, the cultivation of study would involve decluttering our environment and having solitude and silence.[41] Surely, less mess and fewer screens would be conducive to study, but often these physical markers are well ingrained into what makes our house a *home*.[42] Unfortunately, "beholding is easily disrupted by needless chatter and noise (both within and without). Study is nourished by silence and solitude. Yet often uncomfortable with both, we surround ourselves with noise and are easily drawn into chatter."[43] Nevertheless, organizing our desk or living room is going to go only so far: the issue is much deeper and more theological. The move toward study challenges our propensity to avoid focus, with boredom ever lurking in the background. While it seems that we're expertly trained in avoiding boredom, we need to be clear that boredom is "a harbinger of

39. Zina Hitz, *Lost in Thought: The Pleasures of an Intellectual Life* (Princeton: Princeton University Press, 2020), 147. For all my fellow professors, the opening of Hitz's book is worth reading at the beginning of every semester.

40. See Paul J. Griffiths, *Intellectual Appetite: A Theological Grammar* (Washington, DC: Catholic University of America Press, 2009).

41. Gary, *Why Boredom Matters*, 101.

42. To be sure, this is not necessarily gesturing toward some form of minimalism, which at times is well intentioned but can these days read like religion in the worst of ways.

43. Gary, *Why Boredom Matters*, 102–3.

meaning."[44] Thus, instead of seeking to dodge and divert, we should meet it head-on.

According to theologian John Webster, "Christian theological intelligence is exercised in the conflict between the *virtue of studiousness* and the *vice of curiosity*."[45] Fundamental is the fact that becoming virtuous is not accomplished through merely the acquisition of skills and knowledge.[46] Thus, we don't need to simply fine-tune our schedule; rather, we need to come to grips with curiosity and studiousness in terms of vice and virtue.[47] Webster adds, without softening the issue, that we're speaking of our "complicity in inquisitiveness, idolatry, vanity and lying," but this is, nevertheless, *not* the sum of human creatures.[48] Ordered love, which gives proper station to attention, aims us aright.[49]

A key thrust of study is its "well-ordered, temperate enactment."[50] This is far from a flippant, quick, half-attentioned act; rather, Webster claims a kind of life that is "eager, concentrated, taking pains to acquire knowledge."[51] Now we can begin to see the possible overlap between a focal practice and study. What's more, Webster helps settle us in for reading Psalms by writing, "Chief among the intellectual standards of excellence is the requirement that studious dedication of mental powers must so relate to the object of study that the integrity of the object is respected as it comes to be known."[52] This robust description of the activity speaks to many areas of life. With respect to Scripture, especially the book of Psalms, this suggests that a frantic, harried, instrumentalized reading of the Bible for a quick "word for the day" doesn't stack up to Scripture's *integrity*. The Bible

---

44. Gary, *Why Boredom Matters*, 110.

45. John Webster, "Curiosity," in *The Domain of the Word: Scripture and Theological Reason* (London: T&T Clark, 2017), 193 (emphasis added). While Webster seems to ponder a narrow scope of theologians, I'm intentionally widening the frame of reference.

46. Webster, "Curiosity," 193.

47. Webster, "Curiosity," 193.

48. Webster, "Curiosity," 194.

49. On this, see the accessible book by James K. A. Smith, *You Are What You Love: The Spiritual Power of Habit* (Grand Rapids: Brazos, 2016).

50. Webster, "Curiosity," 194.

51. Webster, "Curiosity," 194.

52. Webster, "Curiosity," 194.

is no magic rabbit-foot or some incantation to be mumbled for a more positive day. The attention given to Scripture should match the nature of this holy book.

Study has much to do with desire, and certainly desire for new knowledge is natural to humans.[53] Nonetheless, this desire, as we might expect, needs to be ordered properly. Almost paradoxically, study "bears within it an element of discontent," since one is not satiated prematurely.[54] Curiosity, on the other hand, "terminates on the *surfaces*," like fast food that doesn't fill.[55] One's patient focus continually and carefully attends to the core concerns, which is altogether difficult, given our ease of boredom and distraction.

In the worst of ways, "curiosity gives itself to whatever sources of fascination present themselves, especially if they are novel."[56] It is what Thomas Aquinas calls "a hankering to find out."[57] In contrast, the study of God "is a moved activity of the mind which seeks out and clings to God with intense delight."[58] Moreover, this activity should result in the building up of the church through maintaining faith and proper living.[59] This realization helps us discern more carefully that curiosity rests in the aberrant satisfaction of coming to know something without properly understanding its relation to the Creator or without the result of *charity* to and for the church.[60]

As we see the similarity and confluence of distraction, boredom, and curiosity, Webster adds that the latter "is pervasive" and unfortunately "grievous in its effects."[61] The nearly ubiquitous curiosity is not checked merely by developing new habits or beginning mornings with a meditation routine. Thus, in contrast to well-intended focal practices, cultivation of new habits per se won't do. Providing banks to our rushing river of curiosity comes through the work of the Holy

53. Webster, "Curiosity," 195.
54. Webster, "Curiosity," 195.
55. Webster, "Curiosity," 196 (emphasis original).
56. Webster, "Curiosity," 198.
57. Thomas Aquinas, *Summa theologiae* II-II, q.167, a.1; as cited and translated in Webster, "Curiosity," 198.
58. Webster, "Curiosity," 199.
59. Webster, "Curiosity," 199.
60. Webster, "Curiosity," 199.
61. Webster, "Curiosity," 199.

Spirit. Webster's wisdom is once again worth citing: "Curiosity dissipates the theological intellect by giving itself to whatever enchanting objects catch its fancy. Studiousness is intelligence *concentrated*."[62] The ends of this kind of concentration are the "adoration of God and edification of others."[63] Conversely, curiosity is "selfish."[64] Thus, study has much to do with habit, but habituation shouldn't have undue influence such that the theological reality of "God . . . with us" is misapprehended (cf. Ps. 46:7, 11; Matt. 1:23). With all that in mind, I'm led to ask: How might concentrated intelligence clarify the act of reading Psalms? How could the psalms order our distracted selves? How does the poetry of Psalms scaffold the soul so that the living God both teaches and ministers to us?

Theology, Prayer, Focal Practice

The road this book walks is not easy. "Thinking and speaking well of the God of the Christian gospel involves the rather bruising business of acquiring and practicing certain habits of mind, heart, and will— 'bruising,' because those habits shape the soul as it were against the grain."[65] One of these key habits, I suggest, is reading the book of Psalms. Its poetry will shape our soul for present and future seasons. From Psalms, we learn who God is, how to commune with him, how to anchor our trust in him, and crucially, how to worship him. This habit with Psalms will certainly show cracks and flaws in our practice of faith and our character. But the rehearsal of these great prayer poems is not meant to level us with guilt and leave shame in its wake. Instead, its purpose is to bring us out of foolish, curiosity-laden living and into a wise life of communion with God.

In reading Psalms today, we should be aware that "engagement with God means being sufficiently grasped, disturbed, or troubled by the gospel and its dispute with us, that we are provoked (however

62. Webster, "Curiosity," 201 (emphasis original).
63. Webster, "Curiosity," 202.
64. Webster, "Curiosity," 202.
65. John Webster, "Habits: Cultivating the Theologian's Soul," in *The Culture of Theology*, ed. Ivor J. Davidson and Alden C. McCray (Grand Rapids: Baker Academic, 2019), 131–32.

unwillingly) to learn how to think and live differently."[66] The book of Psalms is a text for such practice. Holy Scripture, perhaps especially its poetry, moves us and shakes us. Psalms poems require our attention; even more, our attention requires them. We live life in a deficit if we don't allow Psalms to capture our imagination. Here is where habits come to play, for we should be people "engaged in the business of inculcating the habits, learning the virtues, and so coming to have [our] . . . life engraved (usually painfully) with a certain 'character.'"[67] A life centered on amusement is antithetical to the life of virtue: we can't suppose maturity and virtue will thrive while we lean into all sorts of comforted distractions and inane daily practices. Yet the path forward is not simply gritting our teeth and trying harder. The formation of our character comes by way of Holy Scripture and through the grace of the Holy Spirit.

We should not confuse the process of development. "There is no technology of the Spirit, no moral or intellectual or even spiritual performance," that will serve as a quick fix.[68] "What there is—much to our disappointment, usually—is *prayer.*"[69] As the poet Malcolm Guite puts it, "Prayer is the school of theology."[70] There is hardly a better way to become adept at praying than practicing Scripture's prayers. In joy and in trial, the psalms teach us to call out to the living God.

This life of virtue, reading, and attention has more to do with "wonder rather than curiosity."[71] The language of Psalms itself captures and compels wonder. The imagination unfurled through poetic language affects us, but this is, nevertheless, a slow work. In fact, a "key characteristic . . . is 'a patient teachability or deference.'"[72] The present book is witness to the slow work of Psalms on the soul. I trust that throughout the book I will persuade at least some that the purpose of Psalms rests on a foundation of poetry. This poetry has

---

66. Webster, "Habits," 133.
67. Webster, "Habits," 136.
68. Webster, "Habits," 143.
69. Webster, "Habits," 143 (emphasis added).
70. Malcolm Guite, *The Word within the Words* (Minneapolis: Fortress, 2022), 44.
71. Webster, "Habits," 145.
72. Webster, "Habits," 146.

a way of getting into our bones as no other language can: the force of its pedagogy should be seen and appreciated.

Structure of the Book

In order to see the road for the rest of the book, I lay out the content of the following chapters. Chapter 2 gives challenge to the pervasive strategy of reading Psalms as story. Often this is done to give yet a third so-called metanarrative of David and/or Israel (the other two metanarratives are Samuel–Kings and Chronicles). This squinted looking at Psalms to find a narrative arc more often than not runs over the poetry of Psalms, rendering the reading of poetry as a necessary glance before moving on to the so-called story. This chapter argues that the book is not primarily a story but poetry; it defends this argument in detail with the wisdom of Athanasius, who considers Psalms to be a book of sweetness.

Chapter 3 brings out the realities of Psalms being poetry and, at the same time, being part of the Christian canon. Both are meaningful. This is where the book starts to make its contribution most recognizable. Rather than living in canonical readings, thematic connections, and vague theological abstractions of biblical themes in Psalms, this chapter wrestles with the idea of Psalms as Scripture's poetry. Poetry qua poetry is a nearly forgotten truth. Thus, this chapter does not rest on an assumption that all who approach Psalms engage it as poetry: instead, it explicitly shows how Scripture's poetry teaches the reader.

Chapter 4 brings the reader into the large living space of Psalms. Different psalms are for different purposes and seasons. We as readers are shaped inside and out by the truth and beauty of these poems. This chapter specifies how various genres of psalms (e.g., historical, lament, and praise) and the fundamental nature of poetry form the reader to live well, with full faith, in all circumstances.

The second part of the book contains ten short chapters (5–14). These chapters span the Psalter. Each one highlights a specific poetic feature, such as metaphor, ambiguity, and paradox, and illustrates how the selected poem leverages that feature to shape the soul of the reader. The final chapters (12–14) draw attention to what the poetry of the Psalms does that prose does not do. For instance, chapter 12 pictures the worship of the living God by all of creation—humans and the so-called inanimate mountains and rivers. At every turn, these chapters show how our love is reordered by the book of Psalms. These chapters read similar to a Psalms commentary in miniature. The difference, however, is that each reading focuses squarely on the poetry of the selected psalm. Thus, a number of aspects of the modern commentary tradition are not discussed.[73] What is more, commentaries tend to neglect the major feature of *Psalms in an Age of Distraction*—namely, the role of biblical poetry in shaping the soul. The meaning, the significance, and the possibilities that stem from poetry remain paramount in this section.

I conclude with an afterword. The purpose is to leave the reader with thoughts for future engagement with Psalms. The afterword offers an appropriate challenge as well as encouragement to the so-called devotional reading of Scripture—that is, to silent and solitary treatment of the biblical text. Furthermore, it outlines and illustrates the need for more public reading and praying of the psalms.

This book is for the nonspecialist. It is designed to be at home in the hands of students and interested readers. Some parts of the book speak to current academic study of Psalms (e.g., chap. 2 below), but on the whole, *Psalms in an Age of Distraction* lays out how the language of Psalms engages the imagination and shapes the soul (chaps. 2–4). A large portion of the book (chaps. 5–14) demonstrates how certain psalms give us words of prayer and praise. The remainder of this book is not meant as an introduction to Psalms or as a primer on poetry; thus, various aspects of Psalms study will not be discussed.[74]

---

73. For instance, I provide no details on text critical matters, history of reception, or canonical criticism.

74. Some key introductions, primers, and contextual readings are Rolf A. Jacobson and Karl N. Jacobson, *Invitation to the Psalms: A Reader's Guide for Discovery and Engagement* (Grand Rapids: Baker Academic, 2013); Patrick D. Miller Jr., *Interpreting the Psalms* (Minneapolis: Fortress, 1986); Alastair G. Hunter, *An Introduction to the Psalms*, T&T Clark Approaches to Biblical Studies (London: T&T Clark, 2011); Robert Alter, *The Art of Biblical Poetry*, rev. ed. (New York: Basic Books, 2011); Adele Berlin, *The Dynamics of Biblical Parallelism*, rev. ed. (Grand Rapids: Eerdmans, 2008); Stephen B. Reid, *Listening In: A Multicultural Reading of the Psalms* (Nashville: Abingdon, 1997).

Instead, I put my finger on the pulse of the psalms and listen. I remain focused on *what the language of Psalms is meant to do* and *how the psalms shape the soul of the reader*. Before listening more closely to Scripture's poetry, let us recall these words:

> Forever, O Lord,[75] your word
>   is firmly fixed in the heavens.
> Your faithfulness endures to all generations;
>   you have established the earth, and it stands fast.
>   (Ps. 119:89–90 ESV)

---

75. Throughout the book, when the divine name (Yahweh) is referenced in a biblical text, the translation, whether my own or some other version (cf. ESV), is "Lord." Outside of biblical quotations, however, I use "Lord."

$-2-$

Not a Story

At the moment, a number of leading voices say that, in some form or fashion, Psalms is a story.[1] At its worst, this reading minimizes and overrides the rich theological language and purpose that reside in the individual poems. As a response, this chapter will show that the book of Psalms should primarily be read in light of the individual beauty, theology, and expression of each psalm.[2] To make this argument, I frame the chapter around the writings of the fourth-century church father Athanasius, specifically drawing out his understanding of the language and intention of Psalms. Above all, I contend that Psalms is what Athanasius calls it: a book of sweetness. I aim for us to savor these rich words so that we—who know the Word, the Christ—are shaped by the poetry that we ponder and pray.

1. The seminal work is G. H. Wilson, *The Editing of the Hebrew Psalter*, SBLDS 76 (Chicago: Scholars Press, 1985). Recent practitioners will be noted throughout the chapter.
2. See F. W. Dobbs-Allsopp, *On Biblical Poetry* (New York: Oxford University Press, 2015); Elaine James, *An Invitation to Biblical Poetry*, EBS (New York: Oxford University Press, 2021).

The Winning Exactitude of Psalms

Psalms, like all of Holy Scripture, is profitable for teaching.[3] From that general observation, Athanasius goes a long way to show how the psalms are *similar* to other biblical texts, especially in the Old Testament.[4] For instance, patriarchs and the exodus appear in the Pentateuch and Psalms; prophecies find purpose naturally in the prophetic books as well as the Psalter.[5] Athanasius highlights more common themes, such as land (Joshua and Judges; cf. Ps. 105), to underscore the pervasive correspondence. He recounts that such "things are sung in the Psalms, and they are foretold in each of the other books of Scripture."[6] Yet that similarity in content serves as a baseline for Athanasius then to expound how Psalms is *different*— and why.

Athanasius writes, "The Book of Psalms is like a garden containing things of all these kinds, and it sets them to music, but also exhibits things of its own that it gives in song along with them."[7] With such a sentence, we gather a sense of just what the distinction between Psalms and other biblical books might be. The psalms are texts filled with imagination, images, and emotion for praying and singing in all stations of life. This *dissimilarity* between Psalms and other scriptural texts proves to be at least part of what shapes the soul of the reader. Psalms as poetry invites us to behold the Lord God in ways that prose texts do not. These poems teach our mind and mouth to learn and speak of God aright.

---

3. Athanasius, *The Life of Antony and the Letter to Marcellinus*, trans. R. C. Gregg, with an introduction by Gregg and a preface by W. A. Clebsch (New York: Paulist Press, 1980), 101. For more on Athanasius and Scripture in general, see Thomas F. Torrance, "The Hermeneutics of Athanasius," in *Divine Meaning: Studies in Patristic Hermeneutics* (Edinburgh: T&T Clark, 1995), 229–88.

4. Scholarly views on Athanasius have shifted over the years, from positive to extremely negative, but at present there appears to be a rather leveled perspective. See Hikaru Tanaka, "Athanasius as Interpreter of the Psalms: His Letter to Marcellinus," *Pro Ecclesia* 21 (2012): 422–47, esp. 424.

5. Athanasius, *Letter to Marcellinus*, 101–2.

6. Athanasius, *Letter to Marcellinus*, 106.

7. Athanasius, *Letter to Marcellinus*, 102; cf. David Willgren, *The Formation of the "Book" of Psalms: Reconsidering the Transmission and Canonization of Psalmody in Light of Material Culture and the Poetic of Anthologies*, FAT 2/88 (Tübingen: Mohr Siebeck, 2016).

Athanasius presses on: Psalms, "possessing the characteristic feature of the songs, itself chants those things in modulated voice that have been said in the other books in the form of detailed narrative, as already mentioned."[8] Athanasius balances content and purpose here; the book of Psalms, to be sure, not only sings but also "legislates," "narrates," and "prophesies"; yet these latter features are minimal in comparison to the poetic, melodic nature of Psalms.[9] On the theme of poetic Scripture, Brian Daley highlights embodiment of the Psalms:

> The driving concern of early Christian exegesis of the Psalter, in fact, seems to have been somewhat different from that which animated the interpretation of other books of the Bible. . . . Its point was not simply to identify the referent of a particular verse or passage, to find the "prophetic" significance of a text for the Christian reader, but to facilitate the *internalization* of these biblical prayers-in-verse, to enable the reader so to feel and grasp them, as works of divinely inspired poetry, that the reader's own thoughts and emotions, desires and passions, might be purified and transformed.[10]

The beauty of opening our own desires to the Lord through prayer is on display in the Psalms. These poems of Holy Scripture both direct and correct our desires by way of the Holy Spirit.

Recent study of Psalms consists, at the very least, of viewing Psalms as a literary book in which psalms are meant to be interpreted in light of their neighboring psalms and the collection in which they reside—but also, crucially, in "a storyline [that] unfolds throughout the book."[11]

8. Athanasius, *Letter to Marcellinus*, 107.
9. Athanasius, *Letter to Marcellinus*, 107.
10. Brian Daley, SJ, "Finding the Right Key: The Aims and Strategies of Early Christian Interpretation of the Psalms," in *Psalms in Community: Jewish and Christian Textual, Liturgical, and Artistic Traditions*, ed. Harold W. Attridge and Margot E. Fassler (Atlanta: SBL Press, 2003), 192 (emphasis original). The point that Daley draws out is in stark contrast to several modern readings.
11. David M. Howard Jr. and Michael K. Snearly, "Reading the Psalter as a Unified Book: Recent Trends," in *Reading the Psalms Theologically*, ed. David M. Howard Jr. and Andrew J. Schmutzer, Studies in Scripture and Biblical Theology (Bellingham, WA: Lexham Academic, 2023), 4. For a more nuanced approach, see Sigrid Eder, "Storytelling in the Psalter? Chances and Limits of a Narrative Psalm Analysis—Shown Exemplarily in Psalm 64," *Old Testament Essays* 32 (2019): 343–57.

The latter unfurls in reading the so-called "Meta-Narrative of the Psalter," the story of "post-exilic survival."[12] The nagging dilemma of viewing the Psalter as story is "Why?" Why does the Old Testament here need *another* long text telling a story—and more specifically, the *same* story? The narratival angst of discerning what it means to be Israel after exile, the focus on Torah, the significance of temple and worship—these are all key features of Chronicles. As such, a Psalter-ed story makes little (if any) contribution.[13]

There is, of course, precedent for textual and thematic overlap. Certainly, the narratives in Chronicles and Samuel–Kings correspond in content, as on David's reign, but the central distinctions between them, their purpose, and their style are not difficult to find. On the other hand, Psalms as story has little to no distinct flavor *as a narrative* when put next to these texts. At this juncture, I admit, nonetheless, that Psalms *can* be read as story; I am just ambivalent as to why it should be read as such.[14] Even if the reading is reasonable, the

---

12. Nancy L. deClaissé-Walford, "The Meta-Narrative of the Psalter," in *The Oxford Handbook of the Psalms*, ed. William P. Brown (New York: Oxford University Press, 2014), 362–68; deClaissé-Walford, ed., *The Shape and Shaping of the Book of Psalms: The Current State of Scholarship*, AIL 20 (Atlanta: SBL Press, 2014); deClaissé-Walford, *Reading from the Beginning: The Shaping of the Hebrew Psalter* (Macon, GA: Mercer University Press, 1997). I need to mention that deClaissé-Walford reads Psalms with careful attention to literary, especially poetic, features. See, for instance, Nancy L. deClaissé-Walford, Rolf A. Jacobson, and Beth LaNeel Tanner, *The Book of Psalms*, NICOT (Grand Rapids: Eerdmans, 2014); deClaissé-Walford, "Psalm 145: All Flesh Will Bless God's Holy Name," *Catholic Biblical Quarterly* 74 (2012): 55–66.

13. I thank Joshua Williams, a scholar of Chronicles, for discussion on this. The arguments and any errors are, however, my own.

14. This is not to mention the struggle among Psalms-as-story scholars who still cannot come to a consensus as to whether David is the main character of the book. In the early days of this canonical reading, interpreters viewed David as giving way to a more democratic wisdom reading of the book. Recently, however, there have been detailed arguments for a Davidic reading of the entire book. Yet I find the debate somewhat comical. As I think of my young sons, teaching them how to read narrative and poetry, I cannot imagine teaching them to read Psalms as a unified story with a plot if I, leaning on the expertise of the most learned, am unsure who the main characters are. Nonetheless, I do not wish to push the point further and will not use the confusion about characters as sufficient evidence for dismissing the Psalms as story. More robust issues with the substance of the so-called storyline appear in the body of this chapter (below).

exegetical and theological contribution appears to me minimal, at best.[15] On this point, it's instructive to recognize that, for the early church, the interpretation of the Psalter "presented distinctive problems for interpretation and called for distinctive strategies: above all, because it is not a book of continuous narrative or instruction but a collection of *poems*."[16]

One strategy in engaging the poetry of Psalms is to acknowledge that the "psalms are . . . sample prayers" and "driven by the conviction that human life is clearly defined as a praying existence."[17] These prayers, irrespective of any specialized genre, are given the label "praises" (*təhillîm* in Hebrew), so as to communicate that each psalm "aims at contributing to God's praise in a comprehensive theological sense."[18] The psalms thus "offer the words."[19]

In unsettling us from curiosity and distraction, the psalms awaken us through "the individuality of every single psalm."[20] Thus, we

15. For further studies on the story of Psalms, see David Gundersen, "A Story in the Psalms? Narrative Structure as the 'Seams' of the Psalter's Five Books," in Howard and Schmutzer, *Reading the Psalms Theologically*, esp. 79–81. Somewhat similar is the attempt to nuance, such as that by Robert E. Wallace, "The Narrative Effect of Psalms 84–89," *Journal of the Hebrew Scriptures* 11 (2011): 1–15.

16. Daley, "Finding the Right Key," 194 (emphasis original).

17. Hermann Spieckermann, "From the Psalter Back to the Psalms: Observations and Suggestions," *ZAW* 132 (2020): 18. See Gianni Barbiero, Marco Pavan, and Johannes Schnocks, eds., *The Formation of the Hebrew Psalter: The Book of Psalms between Ancient Versions, Material Transmission and Canonical Exegesis*, FAT 151 (Tübingen: Mohr Siebeck, 2021), esp. the following chapters: Marco Pavan, "The Psalter as a Book? A Critical Evaluation of the Recent Research on the Psalter," 11–82; David Willgren Davage, "What Could We Agree On? Outlining Five Fundaments in the Research of the 'Book' of Psalms," 83–118; and William Yarchin, "Why the Future of Canonical Hebrew Psalter Exegesis Includes Abandoning Its Premise," 119–38.

18. Spieckermann, "From the Psalter Back to the Psalms," 19.

19. Spieckermann, "From the Psalter Back to the Psalms," 19. In his introduction to Psalms, he adds, "The one who responds to God's love becomes one who prays" (Der Gottes Liebe erwidernde Mensch wird zum Betende). *Psalmen 1–49*, ATD Neubearbeitungen 14 (Göttingen: Vandenhoeck & Ruprecht, 2023).

20. Spieckermann, "From the Psalter Back to the Psalms," 20. For work on the fundamental import of aesthetics and prophetic poetry, see, e.g., Katie Heffelfinger, "More than Mere Ornamentation," *Proceedings of the Irish Biblical Association* 36–37 (2013–14): 36–54; Heffelfinger, "Persuasion, Poetry and Biblical Prophets," *Proceedings of the Irish Biblical Association* 43–44 (2020–21): 38–53. On biblical poetry, see Elaine James and Sean Burt, "'What Kind of Likeness?': The Aesthetic

should welcome "the miracle that psalms have served as texts for praying until today" and, in turn, we should humbly "wonder about the psalms as a unique gift of language enabling human beings to communicate with God in all situations of life."[21]

That is exactly what Athanasius is getting at: the psalms are prayer texts that shape the pilgrims who voice them. The language of Psalms—with all its images, nuance, openness, ambiguity, paradox, and succinctness—is meant to move the prayer (the person praying) internally and externally; each poem shapes the soul. In our modern moment of distraction, this news is both good and disturbing: good in that we're not left to our devices, but disturbing in that our life and loves, driven by spectacle, are wholly reconfigured.

The issue for interpreting Psalms is, above all, one of salience. Which program, the narrative or the poetic, is more significant? Which reading strategy holds more closely to the purpose of the book of Psalms itself? More important for our study: Which should shape the soul of the reader? My argument is not ambiguous: the poetry of Psalms, stuffed with paradox, emotion, and metaphors for every season of the soul, is the mode of reading that shapes the soul.[22] Its sweetness draws us in so that our desires can be molded by and for the living God.

A Certain Grace

Grace pervades all of Scripture. "But even so, the Book of Psalms thus has *a certain grace* of its own, and a distinctive *exactitude of expression*."[23] Athanasius's point needs hearing in the current practice of Psalms reading. Certainly, readers of Psalms are more than

---

Impulse in Biblical Poetry," *Prooftexts* 38 (2020): 1–33. For Psalms specifically, see Elaine James, "The Aesthetics of Biblical Acrostics," *JSOT* 46 (2022): 319–38.

21. Spieckermann, "From the Psalter Back to the Psalms," 21.

22. To my point, Harry Nasuti reflects on Athanasius's reading of Psalms, which "sees the psalms as *doing* something to the person praying, something that happens specifically through the agency of these texts." *Defining the Sacred Songs: Genre, Tradition, and the Post-Critical Interpretation of the Psalms*, JSOTSup 218 (Sheffield: Sheffield Academic, 1999), 111, 116–17 (emphasis original).

23. Athanasius, *Letter to Marcellinus*, 107 (emphasis added).

aware that the book contains poetry, yet this "exactitude of expression" can be lost to a vague storyline. Athanasius's attention to the poetry of Psalms proves to be a corrective for modern interpretation. For example, David Howard and Michael Snearly write, "Reading the Psalter in this way [as a book with a unified message] brings its message into harmony with the rest of the Old Testament, which consistently has a forward-looking bent. The Abrahamic, Mosaic, and Davidic covenants all point ahead to the ultimate covenant, the new one, ushered in by the true 'David,' Jesus the Christ."[24] Crucially, harmony with the Old Testament is never doubted by Athanasius.[25] Howard and Snearly nevertheless claim, "To deny the lasting significance of the Old Testament covenants is to impoverish one's reading of the Psalms and, indeed, one's own life of faith."[26] Again, Athanasius, as well as Augustine and Ambrose, would find little difficulty in agreeing (at least at a general level) on the christological significance of the covenants, specifically as stipulated in Psalms.[27] The poetry of Psalms need not play a secondary role for Psalms to be read theologically.

The way words work in Psalms speaks to and heals passion.[28] The words of these poems can be dulled if the primary aim is finding themes and catchwords that run throughout a series or collection of psalms. The edge of Athanasius's point on Psalms as prayer comes in finding "therapy and correction suited for each emotion."[29] He does not let this argument go, as he writes, "If the point needs to be put

24. Howard and Snearly, "Reading the Psalter," 34.
25. Even more broadly, Brian E. Daley, SJ, recognizes that the "underlying unity in the message of the Bible, definitely revealed to the Christian in the gospel, was generally understood by patristic and medieval interpreters to produce, not a flat uniformity of doctrine, but a new richness and variety, a kind of unquenchable fountain whose scattered drops all reflect the one Mystery of Christ." "Is Patristic Exegesis Still Usable? Some Reflections on Early Christian Interpretation of the Psalms," in *The Art of Reading Scripture*, ed. Ellen F. Davis and Richard B. Hays (Grand Rapids: Eerdmans, 2003), 77.
26. Howard and Snearly, "Reading the Psalter," 34.
27. Daley, "Is Patristic Exegesis Still Usable?," 74. On Athanasius specifically, see Tanaka, "Athanasius as Interpreter," 433; James D. Ernest, *The Bible in Athanasius of Alexandria* (Boston: Brill Academic, 2004).
28. Athanasius, *Letter to Marcellinus*, 108.
29. Athanasius, *Letter to Marcellinus*, 112.

more forcefully, let us say that the entire Holy Scripture is a teacher of virtues and of the truths of faith, while the Book of Psalms possesses somehow the perfect image for the souls' course of life."[30]

Athanasius, claiming that all Scripture inculcates, contends that the anatomy of Psalms is specific and distinct. He outlines how someone can use Psalms effectively in each and every season of the soul. Whether one needs prayer because of opposition or one wants to "celebrate God in song," there is a psalm for both of these moments. Athanasius spends nearly a third of his letter detailing occasions of the soul and psalms that correspond. Such an effort makes sense, as he understands this as what Psalms is actually for: to express the emotions of humanity.[31] Thus, someone can pick up and read one psalm or read through the entirety of the book. No matter the case, the reader will experience the mirrored effect of each psalm because that is the purpose of the poetry. Taking my cue from Athanasius, I argue that reading the psalms for a story, a metanarrative, or highlighting neighboring thematic connections, even if interesting and enlightening, is in fact an afterthought for Psalms exegesis. I am, therefore, trying to make a clear point on salience in Psalms: the individual psalm demands primary attention, however its additional contexts are construed.

What's more, the open language of Psalms encourages readerly engagement in ways that other biblical texts cannot.[32] Athanasius writes, "Things are said, then in close sequence; such are all the contents of the Law and the Prophets and the histories, along with the New Testament. On the other hand, things are expressed more broadly; of this kind are the phrases of the psalms, odes, and songs. For thus will it be preserved that men love God with their whole strength and power."[33] If we were to consider Psalms as analogous to "the histories," we would miss the language of both the histories and Psalms. On the uniqueness of the Psalter, however, Brian Daley brings in

30. Athanasius, *Letter to Marcellinus*, 112.
31. More specifically, emotions are construed in relationship to faith in Christ and worship of God.
32. See, e.g., Patrick D. Miller Jr., "The Theological Significance of Biblical Poetry," in *Language, Theology, and the Bible: Essays in Honour of James Barr*, ed. Samuel E. Balentine and John Barton (Oxford: Clarendon, 1994), 213–30.
33. Athanasius, *Letter to Marcellinus*, 124.

Basil of Caesarea to highlight that "the poetry and music inherent in the Psalms . . . gives [the Psalms] their distinctive power and makes their teaching—which they share with the rest of the Bible—uniquely accessible."[34] The words of Psalms, with its metaphors, lines, and cadence, wrestle with the soul. Order and healing come by way of Psalms, in Athanasius's view: "The harmonious reading of the Psalms is a figure and type of such undisturbed and calm equanimity of our thoughts. . . . The desire of the soul is this—to be beautifully disposed. . . . In this way that which is disturbing and rough and disorderly in it is smoothed away, and that which causes grief is healed when we sing the psalms."[35]

Nevertheless, one similarity between the metanarrative reading of Psalms and Athanasius is an appreciation for the whole of the book. Athanasius comments, "Now, my son, it is necessary for each of the readers of that book to read it in its entirety, for truly the things in it are divinely inspired, but then to take benefits from these, as from the fruits of a garden on which he may cast his gaze when the need arises."[36] The whole of Psalms is readied for the reader to come to when in need. Nonetheless, the *needs*—at least as Athanasius sees them—are not attended to by plotting a storyline that shows the rise and fall of David and the fall (exile) and rise (return) of the people. As important as these historical moments are (cf. Samuel–Kings; Chronicles–Ezra–Nehemiah), that is simply not what the psalms do. Athanasius proclaims, "For I believe that the whole of human existence, both the dispositions of the soul and the movements of the thoughts, have been measured out and encompassed in those very words of the Psalter."[37] Such an interpretation is, on the whole, fairly

34. Daley quotes Basil on this score: "The delight of melody He [the Holy Spirit] mingled with the doctrines, so that by the pleasantness and softness of the sound heard we might receive without perceiving it the benefit of the words, just as wise physicians who, when giving the fastidious rather bitter drugs to drink, frequently smear the cup with honey." Basil of Caesarea, "Homily 10: On Psalm 1," in *Exegetic Homilies: On the Hexameron and On the Psalms*, trans. Agnes Clare Way, FC 46 (Washington, DC: Catholic University of America Press, 1963), 152; cited in Daley, "Is Patristic Exegesis Still Usable?," 81–82.
35. Athanasius, *Letter to Marcellinus*, 125.
36. Athanasius, *Letter to Marcellinus*, 126.
37. Athanasius, *Letter to Marcellinus*, 126.

uncontroversial. The force of Athanasius's words, however, comes in reference to the purpose of Psalms within Holy Scripture. This has everything to do with what we expect when we open up the psalms. The words of Psalms are crucial for the life of the church. Athanasius guides us once more:

> Do not let anyone amplify these words of the Psalter with the persuasive phrases of the profane, and do not let him attempt to recast or completely change the words. Rather let him recite and chant, without artifice, the things written just as they were spoken, in order for the holy men who supplied these, recognizing that which is their own, to join you in your prayer, or rather, so that even the Spirit who speaks in the saints, seeing words inspired by him in them, might render assistance to us.[38]

That is to say, the words of Psalms are kept as they are—not abstracted. Their rationale is to give form and content to the prayers of pilgrims. This is not to dismiss reflecting on the theology of Psalms—whether biblical or dogmatic. Rather, Athanasius helps us differentiate intellectual rumination (including abstracting into narration) from the freight of Psalms. Thus, Athanasius can say, "Reciting even now the same words [of Psalms], let each person be confident, for God will pay heed quickly to those who make supplications through these."[39] The psalms are for pray-ers, for the psalms are prayers, whatever macrostructure of the book one might later find. What is more, given their nature as poetic prayers, any further pursuance beyond the language and theology of prayer should be rendered secondary, if not tertiary.

A Book of Sweetness

I want to conclude the chapter with a summary from Brian Daley on how pre-modern Christians engaged the book of Psalms.

> Early Christian commentators on Scripture were virtually all highly trained in the grammatical and rhetorical skills of classical *paideia*

38. Athanasius, *Letter to Marcellinus*, 127.
39. Athanasius, *Letter to Marcellinus*, 127.

and realized that poetry is a distinctive use of language, designed to speak to the feeling as well as to the mind, to "beguile" or "divert" . . . as well as to inform. A common way of referring to this effect in the ancient world was to speak of the "delight" or "sweetness" that the hearer of poetry was intended to drink in—either as added motivation for taking to heart a poem's intended lesson or simply as a poem's ultimate purpose.[40]

The form of Psalms makes demands on the readers. I suggest that this means a (re)turn to the ever-important art of reading poetry. By that, I am not simply suggesting a quick and general categorization of parallelism ad infinitum, but close attention to the language of poetry in all its fullness. Daley gestures toward the significance of attention to words: "The task of the early Christian exegete, then, was clearly not only a matter of reading the psalms for their content as moral instructions or prophecies or as witnesses to the long divine narrative that would culminate in the story of Christ and the church but also to read them as poems—and that meant using all the analytical tools and theoretical principles that ancient literary criticism . . . had developed for interpreting and judging secular verse."[41] Athanasius recognizes that hearing the psalms brings a degree of understanding that is already in place within Samuel–Kings, Chronicles, Isaiah, and so on. Yet "the Psalter cultivates the emotions."[42]

This chapter has savored the truth that Psalms is a book of sweetness. The poetry drips of honey and helps us taste the good words from the God who is good.[43] The drudgery and hyperactivity that

40. Daley, "Finding the Right Key," 195.
41. Daley, "Finding the Right Key," 196.
42. Athanasius, *Letter to Marcellinus*, 145n25. Paul Koblet summarizes Athanasius on Psalms: "The language of the Psalter progressively 'counters the instability of selfhood' with the stability of a written text that becomes a second nature when it is written in the soul" ("Athanasius, the Psalms, and the Reformation of the Self," *Harvard Theological Review* 99 [2006]: 101, citing Geoffrey Harpham, *Ascetic Imperative in Culture and Criticism* [Chicago: University of Chicago Press, 1987], 41). According to Hikaru Tanaka, "It is striking that Athanasius's reading of the Psalms is governed by Trinitarian connotations and not by any rote technical methodology in order to attempt to obtain some deeper meaning of the Psalms." "Athanasius as Interpreter," 446.
43. See further Christopher R. J. Holmes, *The Lord Is Good: Seeking the God of the Psalter*, Studies in Christian Doctrine and Scripture (Downers Grove, IL: IVP Academic, 2018).

come with boredom and distraction sour the mouth in the worst of ways. Habits of curiosity can cause us to forget the flavor of Scripture's poetry, but once the words are tasted (again), our habits begin to form so that we are shaped by poetic Scripture to pray and praise.[44]

44. At the time of my writing, Brent Strawn was also making similar observations and critiques. According to him, reading "the psalms as poetry, not as stories, is . . . ultimately in service to a better understanding and appreciation of . . . how they strike like a bolt from heaven, into the very heart of the faithful." Strawn, "Too Tall a Tale, Or: Do the Psalms Really Tell 'Stories'?" *Word & World* 43 (2023): 332. Thanks to Brent for drawing my attention to this article.

— 3 —

Poetic Scripture

"All Scripture is breathed out by God and profitable for teaching, for reproof, for correction, and for training in righteousness" (2 Tim. 3:16 ESV). This familiar text reminds us of the source and benefit of Scripture; the following verse lays out Scripture's purpose: that the servant "of God may be complete, equipped for every good work" (3:17 ESV). In practice, readers may take this passage and then aim their attention at the imperatives in Paul's letters, be it Ephesians or Philippians, with some scattered consideration of the Gospels, especially Matthew 5–7. The thought is directive: listen to the commands of Paul, such as "Stand firm" (1 Cor. 16:13) or "Think on these things" (Phil. 4:8); "These are your commands" (cf. 1 Thess. 4:2); "Now go and do them" (cf. 1 Cor. 11:17).[1] Readers and even whole congregations can gravitate toward the to-do kind of texts that allow for more straightforward application in the life of the church.

---

1. In reading a recent and popular book on Christian sanctification, I noticed the author was trying to clarify what *the Bible* teaches about purity. Their evidence for what *the Bible* says is as follows: "Be pure and blameless" (Phil. 1:10), "Keep yourself pure" (1 Tim. 5:22), and "Be self-controlled, pure" (Titus 2:5). In other words, the author appeals first and foremost to Pauline imperatives to detail what the Bible says about purity. See Dane C. Ortlund, *Deeper: Real Change for Real Sinners* (Wheaton: Crossway, 2021), 113.

While it might seem that this prominent passage in 2 Timothy serves as the warrant for such an interpretation, a near-exclusive focus on New Testament texts, particularly ones that major on commands, produces serious problems.

First, in 2 Timothy 3, "Scripture" would primarily signal to Paul's readers what we call the Old Testament. Thus, while we might take the passage as encouragement to continue reading Paul's letters to the exclusion of the Old Testament, the actual heft of the text prompts us to go directly to the Old Testament. Second, a common practice of focusing on biblical texts that have clear and even frequent commands is not necessarily what 2 Timothy 3 is getting at. Evidence for this comes from a quick scan of Paul's letters that quote from, allude to, and echo various Old Testament texts with no command in them. Thus, Scripture does not need to have explicit commands in order to teach, reprove, correct, or train in righteousness—an obvious though underappreciated point.

This leads us to the book of Psalms. First, this book certainly fits within the scope of "all Scripture." Thus, when we peruse it, we are reading the Holy Scripture "breathed out by God." As we read, furthermore, we should be expecting "teaching, . . . reproof, . . . correction, and . . . training in righteousness." Second, while we will find commands throughout the book of Psalms, most often the directives are *from* humans *to* God or *from* the psalmist either *to* his enemies or *to* the congregation. We won't often see God giving explicit commands. Therefore, if these poems are to teach us, they will frequently need to do so without recourse to direct imperatives.

In this chapter, we marvel at the reality of Psalms being *poetic Scripture*. Both words matter. I've already more than hinted that the psalms are from God and are meant to teach: I'll delineate the details of such truths throughout the chapter. What's more, I'll give time and attention to the form and nature of Psalms, especially the relationship of poetry and Scripture. In other words, I want to work out the reality of Psalms teaching, reproving, correcting, and training *differently* than Old Testament narrative or a parable in the Gospels does (cf. chap. 2 above). These psalms, as stated so often already, are poems. This chapter attends to how that rather obvious truth has consequence.

Open Texts

Poetry is hard to unravel. I get it. But what prompts us to think that modern English poetry is hard isn't necessarily applicable for Psalms. Sometimes, poets today revel in the overly complicated layers of linguistic code. For some, it seems, the whole point of writing that kind of poetry is for a reader to respond by saying, "Wow, this poet is a genius. . . . I didn't understand any of it." Again, this is not the case with Psalms.

That's not to say, however, that the poetry of Psalms is swiftly apprehended. This poetry is not some drive-through meal, quickly acquired and rapidly consumed. Psalms is a full meal, thoughtfully prepared, to be savored. In this chapter, I bring home what came up often in chapter 2: the psalms prompt wonder and prayer. The poetry of Psalms is open. By that, I don't mean that any reader can (in reality) take a psalm and make it mean what they want, but poetry as open language entails that the reader is intentionally part of the process, both in reading and in praying.

Take, for instance, the numerous psalms that refrain from naming who the enemies are (cf. Ps. 13). We shouldn't think the psalmist forgot to be specific: the lack of specificity in poetry gives rise to opportunity.[2] Readers can take it up, read, and pray. We can see and say, "Yes, that's like my life too," though, to be sure, the operative word is "like" here: similarity doesn't imply sameness.[3]

This openness has a wide horizon. Some or even many readers would readily take up a handful of psalms for prayer. Other psalms, however, seem a bit too distant, too odd, even too harsh. Most notable would be the so-called psalms of vengeance (e.g., Ps. 137).[4]

2. See esp. Patrick D. Miller Jr., "The Theological Significance of Biblical Poetry," in *Language, Theology, and the Bible: Essays in Honour of James Barr*, ed. Samuel E. Balentine and John Barton (Oxford: Clarendon, 1994), 213–30.
3. On Christian reading(s) of Psalms, see R. W. L. Moberly, *The God of the Old Testament: Encountering the Divine in Christian Scripture* (Grand Rapids: Baker Academic, 2020), 93–124.
4. This is not the place to bring to the fore all my thoughts on this kind of psalm; many a fine theologian and exegete has wrestled with these ideas and texts. The purpose of the present book is not to cover every aspect of Psalms (as an introduction to Psalms would or certainly a commentary must try to do); instead, my eyes are fixed on the scaffolding work of the poetry of Psalms. Some of the more careful

Nevertheless, it is sufficient to note that if the literary nature of Psalms is poetry and its poetry is intentionally equivocal in certain details (both of which are true), then the ideal reader—the one who has faith in the one and only God—is meant to pray and sing along with the "I" and the "we."[5] Remarkably, this is so for all the psalms, not just some of the cherished ones like Psalm 23.[6] So whatever one's view of vengeance in Psalms, we should recognize that these psalms, along with the entirety of the Psalter, evidence the placement of trust and authority in the hands of the living God, *not in the psalmists themselves.*

The openness of the poetry of Psalms allows the reader to walk through the door of the poem and feel at home. Of course, this doesn't dismiss the distance of culture, language, and time, but by anyone's account, Psalms doesn't major on this distance: its language lessens the gap. In doing so, the book itself, by way of the Holy Spirit, is ready to work on its readers. Instructing for a season not yet felt, exhorting in present error, or encouraging in the lowest point of life, the poetry invites us to read, pray, and sing. Below are some examples of how the psalms as open texts provide opportunity for teaching and correction.

---

and theological work on these psalms has been by Frank Lothar Hossfeld and Erich Zenger: for readers of English, see their *Psalms 2: A Commentary on Psalms 51–100,* trans. Linda M. Maloney, Hermeneia (Minneapolis: Fortress, 2005); and *Psalms 3: A Commentary on Psalms 101–150,* trans. Linda M. Maloney, Hermeneia (Minneapolis: Fortress, 2011). See further Stephen B. Reid, "Zion as Problem and Promise: Psalm 137," in *"Wer lässt uns Gutes sehen?" (Ps 4,7): Internationale Studien zu Klagen in den Psalmen; Zum Gedenken an Frank-Lothar Hossfeld,* ed. Johannes Schnocks, Herders biblische Studien (Vienna: Herder, 2016), 360–76; Rodney S. Sadler Jr., "Singing a Subversive Song: Psalm 137 and 'Colored Pompey,'" in *The Oxford Handbook of the Psalms,* ed. William P. Brown (New York: Oxford University Press, 2014), 447–58; Brent A. Strawn, "The Art of Poetry in Psalm 137: Movement, Reticence, Cursing," in *The Incomparable God: Readings in Biblical Theology,* ed. Collin Cornell and M. Justin Walker (Grand Rapids: Eerdmans, 2023).

5. As stated earlier, my purpose in this book is not to lay out all the good and right ways Christians today can and should interpret Psalms. For instance, I won't often discuss in detail the significant christological interpretation of Augustine. In a future project, I hope to bring together the robust theological interpretation of Psalms and its poetic features. For now, however, I focus on the latter.

6. On which, see Richard S. Briggs, *The Lord Is My Shepherd: Psalm 23 for the Life of the Church,* Touchstone Texts (Grand Rapids: Baker Academic, 2021); John Poch, *God's Poems: The Beauty of Poetry and the Christian Imagination* (South Bend, IN: St. Augustine's Press, 2022), 59–67.

Psalm 9 begins with the psalmist declaring thanks and praise (v. 1). The poem soon gives attention to the psalmist's enemies. These nameless folk "stumble and perish" (vv. 3, 5, 6), but verse 7 breaks into theological description: "But the LORD forever sits, having established his throne for justice." As modern readers recite these words, we can learn that enemies aren't the end and that the Lord is indeed King. These poems are not simply ancient musings that cause curiosity: they are words of prayer and praise that teach us today. What's more, we may be addressed when the psalmist speaks to the congregation. "Make melody to the LORD, who dwells in Zion; / tell of his deeds among the peoples" (v. 11). Thus, we can learn from walking in the shoes of the psalmist, but we can also have our hearts directed by receiving the words as the congregation. The openness of the poem offers opportunities for being trained in righteousness in various ways.

Psalm 17 unfolds upon the reader the call for vindication. The psalmist pleads his case to God, but the specifics never surface. Perhaps the psalmist is being maligned ("With their mouths they speak arrogantly," v. 10), but the cause is not altogether clear; I suggest that's intentional. The purpose, as I see it, is not so much to keep the details mysterious, but to prompt readers to pick up and pray *along with* the psalmist. The poem teaches us that we can call on God for vindication in various situations because we're encouraged by Psalm 17 that God hears. Due to the lack of specificity in the poem, modern readers are less prone to distance themselves from the text.

Even when a psalm is situated historically, there are moments when the poetry reaches over the horizon of history and waits for pilgrims to come and pray. Psalm 79 is one such example. The destruction of the temple is the clear conflict:

> The nations have come into your inheritance;
> they have defiled your holy temple;
> they have laid Jerusalem in ruins. (v. 1 ESV)

This event, monumental and nation-altering as it is, is not referential in the life of the reader today. Yet the import of this poem is not wagered on bringing forth historical facts for people to know and perhaps memorize. The angst, confusion, and heartache—all historically laden—teach us more than facts of history. We can grasp the emotions laid out by the psalmist and then say in concert:

> Help us, O God of our salvation,
>   for the glory of your name;
> deliver us, and atone for our sins,
>   for your name's sake! (v. 9 ESV)

Openness exists amid historical detail; this lucidity illuminates the mind of the believer to cry out to God in the most broken and urgent of times. These words of poetry are not meant to be examined as if through glass at a museum; rather, they remain on offer for pilgrims to pray.

Metaphor

Above all, we should read biblical poetry *slowly*.[7] A sauntering read can (and should) be done, whether one is reading Hebrew or English. This suggestion for slowness, of course, has much to do with metaphors. Just think of the form of metaphor itself, the mental picture. It's something intellectually that's within reach, but often it requires sustained reflection. What an amazing tool God uses to help grant understanding, to give opportunity to consider and ruminate and read patiently![8] We typically scan over metaphors quickly, too quickly, ready to move to the next line. But these images, some quite difficult, should help us put on the brake: *Slow down . . . Pause . . . Think.*

Patience is built in: it's part of the process of reading the poetry of Psalms. But we must give ourselves to the actual form and content of Scripture, or else we'll continue to make it an instrument, perhaps even a religious instrument, as if it were a bulleted list of moral to-dos. In attending to the language of Psalms, let's not miss the pedagogical nature of the biblical text, with its many fascinating facets. The metaphors of a deer, a bird, a dog, a walled city, a mother, a father,

---

7. For more on the significance of reading the poetry of Psalms in Hebrew, see my "Forming the Imagination: Reading the Psalms with Poets," *Scottish Journal of Theology* 75 (2022): 329–46.

8. See further Augustine, *De doctrina Christiana*, trans. Edmund Hill (Hyde Park, NY: New City, 2007).

a banquet, a field, and more—all teach us as we see similarities and differences in the figure and the referent. As such, the psalms help us to be less instant and more patient.

Psalm 23, for example, opens with a metaphor that many know: "The LORD is my shepherd" (v. 1). Certainly, the initial frame of the metaphor brings in the agricultural and creaturely world. The psalmist figures himself as a sheep. The import of the shepherding metaphor could easily be care and protection, as several lines in the psalm witness: "grass," "streams of water," and "paths of righteousness" are all due to the shepherd's care. Yet "shepherd" is a multifaceted metaphor in the Old Testament. In Jeremiah 23, the word of the Lord comes against "the shepherds who are causing the flock of his pasture to perish and scatter" (v. 1). In response, the Lord "will raise over them shepherds, and they will shepherd them, and they will not fear again" (v. 4). More specifically, the Lord "will raise for David a righteous Branch; a king will rule and be wise; he will do justice and righteousness in the land" (v. 5). This prophetic passage allows us to see more clearly that shepherding has a royal signification in Scripture. Thus, it's reasonable to suggest that Psalm 23 has a regal frame: to say "The LORD is my shepherd" would then be something like saying, "The Lord is my king."[9] Such recognition comes from reading Scripture with Scripture, all while reading Scripture *slowly*.[10] These figural frames are primed to teach us, but we must give time, attention, and care to allow ourselves to be taught.

Paradox

The book of Psalms being poetry means that paradox is close at hand.[11] Paradox often entails contradiction: poets throughout the ages are

9. See Beth Tanner, "King Yahweh as the Good Shepherd: Taking Another Look at the Image of God in Psalm 23," in *David and Zion: Biblical Studies in Honor of J. J. M. Roberts*, ed. Bernard F. Batto and Kathryn L. Roberts (Winona Lake, IN: Eisenbrauns, 2004), 267–84.

10. See further Ndikho Mtshiselwa, "Context and Context Meet! A Dialogue between the *Sitz im Leben* of Psalm 23 and the South African Setting," *Old Testament Essays* 28 (2015): 704–23.

11. As Bobby Jamieson and Tyler Wittman wisely note, "It is part of Scripture's exactness to be full of paradoxes, especially surrounding the incarnate Son of God,

prone to play with incongruities in language and in the world. But that's not exactly what the book of Psalms does. In Psalms, as with Scripture in general, paradox is a key feature, maintaining "apparent contradiction that ultimately is consistent."[12] For example, "For Jesus to be both God and man seems contradictory but ultimately is not."[13] There is paradox, but it resists superficial contradiction. In terms of literary genre, paradox can appear anywhere, but it's altogether part of the culture of poetry. In order to grasp this feature of psalms poetry, I highlight a few poems below.

The well-known Psalm 46 turns with paradox throughout its poetry. War, peace, and silence pervade the poem. For instance, "Nations rage, kingdoms totter; / he raised his voice—the earth melts" (v. 6). Yet for Israel, "The LORD of hosts is with us; / the God of Jacob is a fortress for us" (v. 7). What's more, the Lord "silences wars to the ends of the earth, / breaking bows and shattering spears" (v. 9). This poem settles in with the paradox of divine protection: "Be still and know that I am God" (v. 10). The way of peace, per Psalm 46, is neither political negotiation nor fighting, but rather recognition of and resting in who God is. The psalm's paradox can correct the saint who views human striving as a premium in life. Lessons lie ahead for the reader who repeats this poem, for God certainly rules Israel, the nations, and indeed the whole world.

Psalm 123 brings together contempt and meekness in a way that might seem counterintuitive. The congregation traces the logic of servants to their master and then says, "Thus, our eyes are to the LORD our God till he has mercy on us" (v. 2). From there, they give a simple call: "Be gracious, O LORD, be gracious, for we have had more than enough contempt" (v. 3). This is at least partially paradoxical: if they have suffered the Lord's contempt to any significant degree, then a steady voice of deference and docility would *not* be the norm—though that's exactly what the community practices in this

---

who is the paradox of paradoxes." *Biblical Reasoning: Christological and Trinitarian Rules for Exegesis* (Grand Rapids: Baker Academic, 2022), 127.

12. Jamieson and Wittman, *Biblical Reasoning*, 138.

13. Jamieson and Wittman, *Biblical Reasoning*, 138. For poetic reflection on this topic, see Malcolm Guite, *Parable and Paradox: Sonnets on the Sayings of Jesus and Other Poems* (Norwich: Canterbury, 2016).

psalm. The very words of the psalm connote servanthood. As such, this poem teaches us how being in turmoil is not definitive for the expression of faith. This psalm in particular trains us in righteousness by seeing rightly the nature of servants and master.

Psalm 127 emphasizes the paradox of work and striving. The premise, which certainly has import in the ancient world, could not be more significant for the modern (Western) reader. Some people "toil," "watch," and "rise early," the psalm says. It seems that these words could come from the marketers of modern distractions, especially if we adjusted the words slightly to "work harder," "hustle," "do one more thing," and so on. But these words are tapping into the nature of humanity, not simply a cultural moment. Importantly, these actions are not necessarily denounced; the psalmist simply puts them in the proper place. "If the LORD does not build, . . . if LORD does not keep, . . . then all is vanity" (vv. 1–2). The modern striving for better, bigger, newer, more productive, and more efficient meets head-on with the reality of the divine. This psalm thus teaches us that pure striving is little more than silliness. The current culture of work is, on the whole, worthless.

The following poem, Psalm 128, assembles two seemingly contradictory concepts, at least as many moderns would have it. The stark contrast is felt most acutely in the NRSVue: "Happy is everyone who fears the LORD" (v. 1).[14] Certainly, we could tease out the full meaning and implications of "happy" and "fear," but the sequence of the words should not be missed.[15] The current impulse for creaturely comfort (cf. chap. 1 above) struggles to make sense of this introductory line of the poem, yet *the happy one*, the one whose feet are set and secure, is the one "who *fears* the LORD." Comfort in terms of modern culture is not the pathway to a flourishing life; the fear of the Lord is.[16]

In all, the paradox of poetic Scripture helps us hold truths in tension. We recognize how the harmony of Scripture may feel like dissonance

14. The ESV reads the contrast with a bit more subtlety for the modern English ear: "Blessed is everyone who fears the LORD."
15. On Ps. 1, see chap. 5 below.
16. Actively searching for discomfort is not intended here. The note is on stability by way of fear of the Lord.

at times, but the poetry puts our ears closer to the music. By such attention, we contemplate the masterful complexity and intention of God's artistry.

Concise Language

The compact, truncated nature of poetry leaves open possibilities for reading. There are intentional gaps that the reader must reckon with, as in the well-known opening to Psalm 23: "The LORD is my shepherd; / I shall not want" (v. 1). The B line, "I shall not want," rests on the A line: because A is true, the psalmist shall not lack. It's a tight, abridged account of God's goodness and care, but the reader needs to put the thoughts together. Words like "so that" and "therefore" only occasionally appear in Psalms. This book of poetry thus teaches us in part by drawing us closer to the words. We need to attend to the lines and the space between, mulling over meaning, implications, and theology.

A similar need to fill the gap occurs in Psalm 31: "In you, O LORD, I take refuge; / let me never be ashamed!" (v. 1). In this short verse rest expectation and theology. The psalmist has a vision of God as safety. Shame, which the psalmist does not wish to experience, is a deeply theological issue in Scripture (cf. Gen. 2:24–25). By seeking refuge in the Lord, the poet anticipates security; otherwise, he would have gone somewhere else for help. These two brief lines that begin the psalm can be read quickly, even hastily. The poetry of Psalms teaches us that riches are found in rumination, particularly in uniting the theology of two compact lines.

Frequently, the second line in psalms poetry brings clarity, specificity, or a concrete sense to what is otherwise metaphorical. In Psalm 39:12, for example, each line increases in specificity and intensity:

> Hear my prayer, O LORD;
>   my cry, give ear;
>   to my tear do not be silent.
> For I am a sojourner with you,
>   an alien like all my fathers!

The verse begins simply with "prayer." Such a word is descriptive enough, but it lacks detail. A prayer could be pitched in any sort of way, with urgency, with reflection, with anger, or with angst. Thus, the move to the next line ("my cry") brings us closer to the internal reality of the psalmist. The prayer is a "cry" rather than a solemn, monotone recitation.

The first line of Psalm 47 follows in the footsteps above. It's reasonably clear with the opening words "All the peoples, clap your hands" (v. 1). Yet the frame of reference is quite wide. Questions such as Why should they clap? necessitate specificity. Such clarity is reached in the B line: "Shout loud to God with a sound of joy" (v. 1). Thus, the clapping and shouting have a divine direction. Reflection on the relationship of these two lines doesn't bring any real twists or turns, but the practice of contemplation readies us for more substantial details.

Take, for instance, verse 8 in the same psalm: "God rules over nations; / God sits upon his holy throne." The symmetry between the two lines is easy enough to see. The B line, however, brings out theological features that should not be missed. The first line tells *what* God does and *where* he does it. The scope of his reign is the nations, those who are beyond the borders of the land gifted to Israel. The B line offers a qualitative view of God's rule: he sits on "his *holy* throne." From this one verse, we start to scratch at the similarity and dissimilarity of divine and human kingship, especially when comparing God's rule to that of human kings of the surrounding nations. God's kingship is a holy one.

Psalm 56 holds the memorable line "What can flesh do to me?" (v. 4 NRSVue). That phrase concludes a string of staccato lines and serves as the crescendo. The movement leading to it is noteworthy. The psalmist first says, "in God, whose word I praise." The poet's attention moves from God's word to God himself in the next line: "In God I trust"; this trust receives detail with the next phrase: "I shall not be afraid!" The logic here isn't explicit. We are meant to put the lines together: the psalmist puts his trust in God; *therefore*, he will not be afraid. The starkness of the juxtaposition, however, helps to instruct. Instead of logical moves made obvious, the poetry stays tight and succinct, encouraging readerly engagement in how the words relate. This mode of poetry recalls the observation by Susan

Gillingham: "Perhaps to learn the art of reading biblical poetry is but a precursor to learning the art of 'doing' theology at all."[17] In Psalm 56, the poetry is building to the final line: "What can flesh do to me?" The last line draws us back to "trust . . . in God"; in so doing, we catch a vision of the psalmist's theological imagination. If he rests in the protection of God, the authority and strength of fleshly humanity pale in comparison. The force of this theological reflection comes in the clothing of prayer poetry.

Psalm 67 stretches for clarity and scope in rich and refreshing ways with the opening verses:

> O God, be gracious to us,
>   bless us;
> make your face to shine with us,
>   to know in the land your way,
>   in all the nations your salvation.
> May peoples praise you, O God,
>   may all the peoples praise you! (vv. 1–3)

This psalm moves from general to specific and back again. The call for blessing swirls around with salvation and praise among Israel and the surrounding nations. The reverberations of blessings are felt well beyond Israel's borders; the stacking together of these poetic lines helps to unveil this theological truth.

Another clarifying juxtaposition comes in the first verse of Psalm 74: "Why, O God, have you spurned us continually? / Your anger smokes against the flock of your pasturage" (v. 1). This full and complex relationship of lines moves us to consider God as one who has slighted Israel. The relationship is explicitly indexed in the B line through metaphor: Israel is the flock, and the Lord is their shepherd. Unlike Psalm 23, the community criticizes the Lord's abdication of shepherding, yet it does so in a way that might elicit sympathy. By framing themselves as sheep without a shepherd, they underscore their vulnerability. This outlining of the situation sets up the plea in the following verse: "Remember your congregation" (v. 2)!

---

17. Susan Gillingham, *The Poems and Psalms of the Hebrew Bible*, Oxford Bible Series (Oxford: Oxford University Press, 1994), 278.

Lines in Psalms are significant for building meaning and tension. The reader often leaves the first line with a hunch, and this gives opportunity for the poet to make theological moves. The psalmist can fill in the gap or stretch the meaning of the first line even further. The poet can also pivot and summon something unexpected in order to arrest attention. In any case, reading and praying the poetry of Psalms means letting each line stack up in our mind to allow the beauty and truth of Scripture to unfold as the Holy Spirit teaches us.

Emotions

Poetry is emotional language. An unfortunate characterization of poetry is that poets simply emote. In other words, poetry is nothing other than writing out their mental processing of life, a linguistic therapy of sorts. While some poetry certainly fits that mold, much poetry throughout the centuries is emotional without being a pure act of emoting. The poetry is doing something more than allowing the poet to get something off his chest.

Giving detail and precision to emotions in Psalms is not an easy task. Cultural, historical, and language differences prove the task to be difficult.[18] Yet we can observe regular and pitched emotions throughout the book of Psalms. Some persistent emotions of the psalmists are frustration and desperation. For instance, Psalm 13 begins with "How long, O LORD? Will you forget me forever?" (v. 1). Or Psalm 22 leads off with "My God, my God, why have you forsaken me?" (v. 1). A similar note of distress is found in Psalm 35: "How long, O LORD, will you go on looking? / Rescue me from their destruction, my precious life from the lions!" (v. 17).

The psalms are prayers of joy and confidence. The famous Psalm 23 rings with a sense of assurance: "The LORD is my shepherd; I shall not want" (v. 1). Though the darkest moments seem to overtake the psalmist, he declares: "I will fear no evil, for you are with me" (v. 4). A table of victory is credited to the living God, as the psalmist

---

18. See, e.g., the recent work by Erin Villareal, *Jealousy in Context: The Social Implications of Emotions in the Hebrew Bible*, Siphrut 27 (University Park, PA: Eisenbrauns, 2022).

says: "You set a table before me, in the presence of my enemies"
(v. 5). Assurance within the poem shines through the darkest of night.

Joy pervades the poetry of Psalm 47. This is evident not only by
the appearance of the word "joy" but also by the content throughout
the entire poem. As noted above, it opens with the call "Clap your
hands, all peoples; / shout to God with loud songs of joy!" (v. 1). The
following verse gives the reason: "For the LORD, the Most High, is
to be feared, / a great king over all the earth" (v. 2). A similar call for
joyous praise appears in verse 6: "Sing praises to God, sing praises; /
sing praises to our King, sing praises!" As before, the reason follows:
"For God is the King of all the earth; / sing praises with a psalm!"
(v. 7). Such joy bubbles over in Psalm 66 as well. It begins with "Shout
for joy to the LORD, all the earth" (v. 1), and reaches even further
heights: "All the earth worships you and sings praises to you; / they
sing praises to your name" (v. 4). The call is "Come and see what
God has done; / he is awesome in his deeds toward the children of
man" (v. 5). The affect of joy in these psalms makes it hard (though
not impossible) for us to read with clenched teeth, furrowed brow,
and stoic monotone.

"Delight" is interspersed throughout the book of Psalms. The
opening psalm contrasts the "wicked, . . . sinners," and "scoffers"
with the one whose "delight is in the instruction of the LORD" (1:1).
The poem gives detail to delight in the following line: "and on his
instruction he meditates day and night" (v. 2). Similar is Psalm 112:
"Praise the LORD! Blessed is the one who fears the LORD; / on his com-
mandments he delights greatly" (v. 1). Psalm 35 shows a reciprocity
of emotion: "The ones *who delight* in my righteousness shout and
rejoice and say continually, / 'The LORD, *who delights* in the peace
of his servant, is great'" (v. 27). Both the congregation and the Lord
delight. A similar exchange is noticed when Psalms 40 and 41 are
read in juxtaposition. The former reads, "To do your will, O God, *I
delight*; / your instruction is in my inner parts" (40:8). The latter ar-
ticulates the psalmist's perspective of the divine: "By this I know that
you delight in me, / that my enemy doesn't cheer over me" (41:11).
Delight is part of the divine life and the life of the disciple.

Fear is a frequent and complex emotion throughout the Psalter.
Early in the book is the call "Serve the LORD with fear" (2:11). The

great Psalm 19 gives a gloss of the *"fear* of the Lord": it "is pure, always standing; / the judgments of the Lord are true; they are righteous altogether" (v. 9).[19] A different sense comes through in the confidence of the psalmist in Psalm 23: "Even though I walk through the valley of the shadow of death, I will *fear* no evil, / for you are with me; your rod and your staff comfort me" (v. 4). Similarly, Psalm 27 opens with "The Lord is my light and my salvation; / whom shall *I fear?"* (v. 1). Psalm 67 gives us a wide vision with the blessing "God shall bless us; / let all the earth *fear him"* (v. 7). Psalm 103 invites adoration of the living God by reflecting on the reality that "as high as the heavens are above the earth, / so great is his steadfast love toward those who *fear him"* (v. 11). Fear is a rich and complicated emotion that Psalms can hold as resourceful as well as antithetical to walking in faith.

The book of Psalms, of course, contains many more emotions than can be noted here. What is fundamentally important for reading the poetry of Psalms today is that the reader not isolate or distance emotions, whether it's the roar of "Let everything that has breath praise the Lord" (150:6) or the cry from one who is "poor and needy," calling for the Lord to "gladden the soul of your servant" (86:1, 4). Engaging the poetry of Scripture means giving all of ourselves, for we are never merely brains-on-a-stick, as the psalms so beautifully and at times painfully show. This, however, isn't an invitation for unbridled emotional expression, but an opportunity for our emotions to be taught by the psalms.

Sacred Truth

The Bible is *about* God. This seems to be uncontroversial, yet our reading habits and expectations may unintentionally go against the grain. We can easily train our minds and eyes to assume that the Bible is foremost about us. Thus, when we pick it up, we may well be thinking, "What can I do differently or better today?" This is not unlike some encouraging words of self-help that are easily accessible

19. For further considerations, see Brent Strawn, "What Is It Like to Be a Psalmist? Unintentional Sin and Moral Agency in the Psalter," *JSOT* 40 (2015): 61–78.

in books or social media today. While the Bible may move us to adjust our behavior, that's certainly not its main purpose. First and foremost, it shows us *who God is*. This is true from Genesis to Jeremiah, from Romans to Revelation. So when we come to Psalms, we need to be ready to (re)consider who God is and what God does, for the book is *about* the Lord God.

Such a truth finds corroboration throughout the Psalter. In Psalm 11, the psalmist laments his situation; as he does so, he reflects on both his past experience with God and simple yet profound theological truths, such as "The LORD is in his holy temple; / the LORD, in the heavens is his seat" (v. 4). Furthermore, "His eyes look, / his eyelashes test the sons of man" (v. 4). "The LORD causes blazing coals to rain on the wicked" (v. 6), "for the LORD is righteous; / he loves righteousness" (v. 7). Though distress runs throughout the poem, the reality of God is named and described by the psalmist.

Similarly, Psalm 20 speaks of God's acts for the majority of the poem. "May the LORD answer, . . . stretch out help, . . . remember, . . . give, . . . fill" (vv. 1–6). The requests rest in verse 6: "Now I know that the LORD has delivered [delivers] his anointed." Certainly, the description of the divine actions is not abstract: it is grounded in God's relationship with the human king of Israel, God's "anointed" (v. 7), but God is at the center of the poem.

Psalm 24 welcomes the reader to the truth that "the earth is the LORD's and its fullness, / the world and the ones dwelling in it" (v. 1). Creation is the Lord's domain (vv. 1–2). Thus, a reasonable question is "Who can ascend the mountain of the LORD? / Who can rise in his holy place?" (v. 3). The answer challenges the reader to a life of purity, seeking the face of the Lord (vv. 4–6). The latter portion goes on to invite "the King of glory" to come in (v. 7). Questions and responses fill the final lines: "Who is this King of glory?" (v. 8) leads to the answer "the LORD, strong and mighty" (v. 8); "the LORD of hosts, he is the King of glory" (v. 10). This poem is about the glorious, strong, Creator God, who is to be worshiped by a community defined by integrity.

Recalling our opening passage from 2 Timothy, these psalms are above all *from God*. This holy frame matters in that they are Scripture and not simply creative reflections of people of faith. What's more, the psalms are *to* God in that they are prayers. Many psalms come from a place of distress and need. Thus, it's unsurprising that the first line of many poems is directed to the *Lord*. A string of similar psalms appears early in the book. Psalm 4 reads, "Answer me, O God of my righteousness!" (v. 1). The following psalm begins with a direct plea: "Give ear to my words, O LORD; / discern my groanings" (5:1). Psalm 6 opens with "O LORD, not in your anger rebuke me, / and not in your wrath discipline me" (v. 1). The next poem grounds the plea in the past: "O LORD, my God, in you I have taken refuge; / save me from all the ones who pursue me and deliver me" (7:1).[20]

In an entirely different tone, Psalm 138 begins with thanksgiving addressed directly to the Lord: "I will give thanks to you with all my heart; / before gods I make melody to you" (v. 1). The familiar opening line of Psalm 139 reads, "O LORD, you have searched me and know; / you know my sitting and rising" (vv. 1–2). The beautiful beginning of Psalm 145 is directed to the living God: "I will extol you, O my God and King, / and bless your name forevermore" (v. 1). These psalms help us recall that the poems are *to* God as well as *from* and *about* him. This means that the richness of the poetry cannot be held as mere emotive musing: as the fullness of the book of Psalms shows, the poems are in so many ways *theological and poetic.*

This chapter has explored some of what is basic to poetry and inherent to Scripture. In other words, we have seen how the openness of poetry, its imagery, its paradox, its concise form, and its proclivity toward strong emotions are all taken in as part of Scripture—"for teaching, for reproof, for correction, and for training in righteousness" (2 Tim. 3:16 NRSVue).[21] In light of the reality of Scripture's poetry discussed in this chapter, the following chapter explores forms and themes that are *specific* to psalms poetry. The purpose is not to survey the book of Psalms exhaustively but to see and feel how the particulars of psalms poetry scaffold the soul.

---

20. See also Pss. 17:1; 22:1; 25:1; 26:1; 27:1.
21. In this chapter, I haven't exhausted the features of poetry. I present various poetic elements in section 2 (chaps. 5–14 below). My task there is to show the pedagogical force of these features, their shaping function.

— 4 —

A Scaffold for the Soul

Life finds us. No matter how good a day we're having, no matter how terrible we think it is, life moves and turns. Of course, life's difficulties are on a spectrum, and losing one's wallet is not the same as losing one's beloved pet. Yet with this scale in mind, it's stunning how small a thing can frustrate our spirit. It's as if every day we're simply waiting to see how soon things go awry. That's life, but in a real sense, that's far from the life to which Psalms invites us. This chapter details *how* the psalms work. We explore the form, content, and purpose of the Psalm's variegated beauty. In chapter 3, we looked at what is common to poetry in *general* and how Psalms uses those qualities to instruct. In the current chapter, our eyes are set on the *specific* features of Psalms poetry that offer us the words to speak in this "praying existence."[1]

Pain and Prayer

As we begin reading, we listen for the interconnection between life's pain and the psalms. Glancing at this biblical book, our minds are

1. Hermann Spieckermann, "From the Psalter Back to the Psalms: Observations and Suggestions," *ZAW* 132 (2020): 18.

quickly flooded with images and words that express pain, grief, sorrow, struggle, crying, sleeplessness, worry, anxiety, and more. A majority of the poems within the book of Psalms are called laments.[2] A lament is a kind of psalm in which the psalmist sizes up the situation, describes it to God, then asks, begs, and pleads for the Lord to remedy the situation, all while typically expressing trust in or promising to praise God.[3] Perhaps portions of this kind of psalm are familiar—"How long, O LORD?" (Ps. 13) or "My God, my God, why have you forsaken me?" (Ps. 22)—but let's think more deeply on how lament psalms form our experience and theology.

First, lament psalms instruct us to live life with eyes wide open.[4] This is a challenge, especially given the distraction, boredom, and curiosity that dominate our lives. If we're constantly looking down at our phones and scrolling aimlessly, then we make it quite hard on ourselves to observe life's details. While we might be able to pop off a text such as "I'm so anxious" or "I can't sleep," our lack of observation of life makes such statements unnecessarily thin. Put differently, we don't often notice what's actually provoking restless nights. This lack of attention is unequivocally not the case with Psalms. Though it's true that most psalms lack specificity about the situation that gives rise to them (recall chap. 3 above), that doesn't mean laments are just generalized grump fests, with no eye on what's happening.

Often laments describe the pains of the psalmists and how they are doing—typically not well, by the way. Laments detail the poets'

---

2. See further Walter Brueggemann, *The Message of the Psalms: A Theological Commentary* (Minneapolis: Augsburg, 1984); Carleen Mandolfo, *God in the Dock: Dialogic Tension in the Psalms of Lament*, JSOTSup 357 (Sheffield: Sheffield Academic, 2002).

3. On lament and the various genres in Old Testament poetry in general, see Elaine James, *An Invitation to Biblical Poetry*, EBS (New York: Oxford University Press, 2021), 76–105; William H. Bellinger Jr., "Psalms and the Question of Genre," in *The Oxford Handbook of the Psalms*, ed. William P. Brown (New York: Oxford University Press, 2014), 313–25; Stuart Weeks, "Form Criticism: The Limits of Form Criticism in the Study of Literature, with Reflections on Psalm 34," in *Biblical Interpretation and Method: Essays in Honour of John Barton*, ed. Katharine J. Dell and Paul M. Joyce (Oxford: Oxford University Press, 2013), 15–25.

4. Cf. Anastasia Boniface-Malle, "How Can We Sing the Lord's Song in Africa?," in *Out of Place: Doing Theology on the Crosscultural Brink*, ed. Jione Havea and Clive Pearson (London: Routledge, 2014), 202–23.

experiences of the pain. Psalm 3, for instance, states in the first line, "How many are my foes? / Many are rising against me" (v. 1). These enemies mock the faith of the psalmist (v. 2). Similarly, Psalm 6 declares, "My eye has become dark from vexation; / it grows weak from all my foes" (v. 7). I want to be careful here that though laments frequently describe the reason the psalmists struggle, it is not the same thing as saying, "We should all be able to look at the pain in our lives and then rationalize the exact reason [or purpose] of that pain"— not even close. The book of Job goes a long way in disabusing us of such a notion. With these parameters in mind, laments help us look around, recognize the situation, name the pain, and begin to cope.

Second, laments check us. We have to wrestle with our vision of God and ourselves. It's self-evident that we all have to deal with pain and suffering of some kind—social, physical, emotional, and so on. Laments push us. If we're not careful, we may begin to think that we ourselves can take care of certain disasters and distresses. We can handle the small and medium-sized stuff, we might think, and God can take care of the big things in life. Put concretely, we can take care of the situation if someone maligns us or smears our name, but if someone is seriously ill, then we're apt to pray for them. Why is that? Is that the vision of life the psalms paint? As you can imagine, the answer is a resounding no!

Laments bring us to the realization that we can't do life on our own. This theological truth shines its light throughout the Psalter. Whether it's the declaration of God as Creator or a plea for resolution in the psalmist's life, God is always center stage.[5] The intersection of God's care for and power over the psalmists encourages the many images for God in Psalms, including God as "rock" or "shield." Laments, therefore, should both constrain and calm us, reminding us that we can't actually see ourselves through a situation on our own, but the living God is the one who can deliver us.

The relationship between lament and trust is not hard to see. We need to trust that God can hear us. We must be confident that he actually cares about what he hears. Then we have confidence that he

5. For a recent work on the theology of Psalms, see Robert L. Foster, *We Have Heard, O Lord: An Introduction to the Theology of the Psalter* (Lanham, MD: Lexington Books/Fortress Academic, 2019).

can do something about it. Every step is steeped in trust. As such, expressing lament is a declaration that we can't navigate life alone. But laments challenge us in yet another way. This one is a little more subtle, a smidgen more religious. I've seen this in my life and the lives of others. When the weight of life hits us, and does so harshly, we might—in an attempt to be holy, in the hope of following God well—try to shift the conversation away from us. In some respect, this is a good and right thing, but let's not move too quickly. One attempt to deflect attention from ourselves comes in the line "Well, it's so much worse for somebody else," and here's where it gets sticky: that's likely true. With constant access to all the world's news, who would contend that personal struggles are on the same level as a people group being exiled, their towns plundered, and their people murdered? This leads to the half-considered thought, "Who am I to worry God with my little situation?"[6] Yet again, lament psalms move us into a different line of thinking.

The idea of comparing pain, struggle, and loss with others' trials seems to be a modern concept, not prevalent within Holy Scripture.[7] Thus, the thought of dismissing our struggles because someone else has it worse is off the point. Laments train our thoughts, prayers, and overall disposition to life. Simply put, God cares! The Lord has deep concern for those people who have experienced the worst of humanity, but he also cares about the seemingly insignificant thing that sends us into an emotional tailspin. Comparison may be the lifeblood of social media, but it's not common in the psalms' treatment of misery.

Sing Praise

Beyond instructing our hearts to cry out to God when in need, the psalms teach us to praise.[8] Such an action is complicated these days. First, there's the trouble with trophies. By that I refer to something in

6. To be sure, though, I'm not comparing someone not liking a social media post with the exile of a people group.
7. Interestingly, Ps. 73 explores comparison in detail and serves as a corrective for myopic adjudications (see chap. 11 below).
8. See Travis J. Bott, "Praise and Metonymy in the Psalms," in Brown, *Oxford Handbook of the Psalms*, 131–46; Erhard S. Gerstenberger, "Petition and Praise:

the cultural waters signaling to us that nearly everyone should receive some kind of adulation: the participation-trophy idea. Hence, the center of praise may well be ourselves rather than our Maker. This seems to underscore our nature as praise-seeking creatures.[9] Second, our vision of church worship has forced our eyes (at least some of us, anyway) in a specific, if not peculiar, direction. It is not uncommon to walk into a church building and hear only rather happy, upbeat praise music. While that might seem to be a good thing, I suggest that it's altogether problematic.

In having loud, exciting, so-called praise music throughout a typical church service, our hearts can become attuned to certain entailments rather than the purpose of praise. In other words, we can come to think that a feeling of happiness or excitement is crucial for bringing praises to God. To be clear, though, I doubt that many people do this knowingly; it's simply a reminder that habits matter.[10] Coming back to Psalms specifically, this book of poems doesn't call us to get happy or excited *in order to* praise God. The reason is plain: praise is not about us or our circumstances, but about God himself.

Here we need to pause for a moment. I'm going to hold on to another thread from the above discussion. Our musical tastes can not only narrow our frame of praise; they can also displace lament. Again, if we're only or primarily accustomed to a certain sense of happiness, then when we join a congregation to sing, week by week we're (unintentionally) instructed to quiet the pain, the sorrow, the struggle. "Get happy, . . . sing, . . . move on," we begin to think. I don't say this to be unduly harsh about a certain kind of music; far from that. I say it because the psalms prompt us to think clearly about ourselves, our surroundings, and—most importantly—God. In order to lament and praise well, we need to draw our attention to the triune God. Our specific mood on a given day is beside the point.[11]

Basic Forms of Prayer in Babylonian and Hebrew Tradition," *Die Welt des Orients* 49 (2019): 81–94.

9. See also the comments by Alan Jacobs, cited in chap. 1 above.

10. See further James K. A. Smith, *Desiring the Kingdom: Worship, Worldview, and Cultural Formation* (Grand Rapids: Baker Academic, 2009); Smith, *Imagining the Kingdom: How Worship Works* (Grand Rapids: Baker Academic, 2013).

11. This is not the same as saying that one's feelings are irrelevant.

In our moments and movements, we can slowly push ourselves into the center of our world and become the capstone of our own thinking. Thankfully, the psalms move us in the opposite direction. The subject matter of Holy Scripture is the object of our praise.[12] That is to say, we fix our eyes on the holy God. Praise psalms differ from other kinds of psalms: praise is not particularly contingent on what God has done for me and you; rather, it is given primarily because God is who he is.[13] Psalm 33 says, for example, "For the word of the LORD is upright, / and all of his work is in faithfulness" (v. 4). Psalm 47 opens with a call for all peoples to clap their hands and shout, "for the LORD Most High is awesome, / a great king over all the earth" (v. 2). Take the famous Psalm 100 as another example that issues a call for shouting, worship, and praise, "for the LORD is good; his steadfast love is forever, / and from generation to generation his faithfulness" (v. 5).

Who God is—that alone, described in various ways throughout the Psalter—substantiates the predicate. There's no need to ask in this case, "What has God done in my life lately?" Certainly, that's not an altogether bad question (though it could use some refinement), but the question is instead, "Who is God?"[14] It might sound simple, too simple, to ask that question. But it's a question that has been asked for millennia. To get at a proper answer, our method matters. For instance, we'd be remiss to gather all we can from the natural world and surmise who God is from there. We'd find nothing but thorns and thistles if we were to pontificate on what a human is and then reify exactly what God is like. Instead, we open our eyes to the teaching given in Holy Scripture to see who God is.[15] This is not anti-historical, anti-nature, and so forth. Instead, it centers on the revelation of God's Word as the means by which we know who God is.

---

12. See further John Webster, *The Culture of Theology*, ed. Ivor J. Davidson and Alden C. McCray (Grand Rapids: Baker Academic, 2019); Webster, *The Domain of the Word: Scripture and Theological Reason* (London: T&T Clark, 2014).

13. Rolf A. Jacobson and Karl N. Jacobson note that these praises "can be sung in both good times as well as bad, [and] we can at least say that the hymn *does not assume a time of crisis*." *Invitation to the Psalms: A Reader's Guide for Discovery and Engagement* (Grand Rapids: Baker Academic, 2013), 47 (emphasis original).

14. Here is a distinction between thanksgiving and praise.

15. See, e.g., Katherine Sonderegger, "The Bible as Holy Scripture," *Pro Ecclesia* 31 (2022): 127–41.

In the denominational tradition of which I'm a part, it's quite common to hear and be challenged with straightforward imperatives: "Go home and read your Bible!" By that, one typically means, "Go home, grab your Bible, and read silently, alone."[16] This is good as far as it goes, but praise psalms sober us to the reality of God. Thus, checking off a daily Bible reading is necessarily incomplete, insufficient, and at best a halfway point. We should (must!) move from reading and reflection to *praise*, directing our life, our knowledge, and our words to God.

Praise shapes and structures our lives. Walking around worried, fixated on our own schedule, and brooding about our own problems won't suffice. Praise itself makes space in our lives, irrespective of disposition or surroundings; we need to be cautious in associating happiness and excitement with praise. Praise doesn't diminish our present moment but instead nudges us, perhaps even prods us, to look *above* our situation for the moment so as to praise Father, Son, and Holy Spirit. The singular focus, not to the exclusion of lament, is that we praise.

The King and Kingdom

God is King. He rules and he reigns: this the heartbeat of Christian confession.[17] While it's not surprising to find this truth in the New Testament, it might catch us by surprise that it is a frequent and central claim within Psalms. Noticeably, such a refrain appears in what's been called the theological heart of the Psalter: book 4 of Psalms.[18] I'd like to consider how these psalms give shape to the soul.

First, these proclamations appear in psalms likely composed when Israel did not have a physical, human king on the throne. Thus,

---

16. I speak more to this in the afterword below.

17. See, e.g., Thomas R. Schreiner, *The King in His Beauty: A Biblical Theology of the Old and New Testaments* (Grand Rapids: Baker Academic, 2013).

18. Book 4 comprises Pss. 90–106. On these psalms, see Bruce K. Waltke and James M. Houston, *Psalms as Christian Praise: A Historical Commentary* (Grand Rapids: Eerdmans, 2019). For discussion on the reception history as it relates to theology, see Susan Gillingham, "Psalms 90–106: Book Four and the Covenant with David," *European Judaism: A Journal for the New Europe* 48 (2015): 83–101.

exclaiming "God is King!" puts hope in the air. Things may have been going awry, and the vision of the kingdom of God might have been blurred due to not having a Davidic king; yet as a resounding force, the psalms give vocal testimony to a watching world and a weak heart: "God is King!" This, of course, pivots nicely to the New Testament by way of theme and history. More than once, the New Testament frames its audience as exiles awaiting restoration and return.[19] When looking around, whether in the first century or the twenty-first, we can see a world violently governed by kings, lords, and rulers. In turn, we could surmise that this globe is far off from God's care, concern, and, importantly, his administration. These psalms step into such dark realities and shine a light. The initial hearers of Psalms and 1 Peter, for instance, are instructed that all is not lost, that this world isn't spinning in chaos. We are tethered to hope by the truth of God's reign.

Second, the psalms confess God's kingship in the context of judgment.[20] This may hit us differently. For some who prefer the rather nice and mostly individualized psalms, say Psalms 23 and 51, these corporate declarations that intermix God's reign and God's judgment are perhaps not the most enjoyable. At some level I understand that, yet we would do well to hear the words of Ellen Charry on the Lord's mocking of the rebellious in Psalm 2: "Personal religious taste is seconded, not for the well-being of the individual, . . . but for the sake of God's universal reign."[21] The news of God's kingship is good in that he makes all things right. It is evident from lived experience and the testimony of Holy Scripture that many rebel against God's gentle and righteous rule. Those of us who have faith in the triune God should not forget that once we were rebels.[22] For God to bring his judgment on and against an unruly world gives testimony to his care and dominion. This has the opportunity to address some of the darkest cellars of the soul.

---

19. I don't wish to highlight every nuanced difference between the initial audience of Psalms, 1 Peter, and Christians today. Instead, here I focus on what is common.

20. See esp. Pss. 96 and 98.

21. Ellen T. Charry, *Psalms 1–50*, Brazos Theological Commentary on the Bible (Grand Rapids: Brazos, 2015), 9.

22. See Rom. 1–2.

It doesn't take much to realize that things are not fine in the world today. Any glance at an online post or news story quickly reminds us of human atrocities. People respond differently to the intake of the world's news. Some might just despair, lamenting (though hardly in the biblical sense) about how bad things are. They may be longing deeply for an imagined time and place long ago, where everything seems (in their perception, at least) to have been fine.[23] Others may take a more active approach. Build a coalition, grow a group, make a stand. In short, do something! These people tend to be the politically affiliated, the ones who in their worst moments of logic think that if their leader, their candidate, their person gets the desired seat of power, then all things will be right. In any case, these (forgive my slight caricature) are people inviting profound disappointment into their lives. No imagined past or rallied future will actually make things right, in the fullest sense. This is not to say that things cannot get better—of course, they can. I'm merely emphasizing social improvement does not equal God's shalom.

Declaring God's kingly judgment outlines a world of peace in both mind and mouth. God puts things right: those who are wicked and rebellious will be held to account. Lest we forget, the opening poem, Psalm 1, often referenced to highlight the good life or the necessity of reading Scripture, actually ends on this very note: "The way of the wicked will perish" (v. 6). My observation is that people (in the most general sense) either don't notice the last line or don't care. Yet this final line helps us hear the music in the rest of the Psalter and, indeed, throughout the whole Bible.

These psalms go to work on us. We're reminded that rebellion has consequences and that chaos doesn't reign. As mentioned, neither nostalgia nor political force should be *the* answer. Such moves don't take stock of the past, the present, and the future. There's an important underlying logic here: announcing that God rules is professing that we do not. Therefore, any lasting, true, and holy consequence is attributed to God. Hearing these scriptural poems and singing these songs, our hearts are secure against the floods of life.

23. See also James K. A. Smith, *How to Inhabit Time: Understanding the Past, Facing the Future, Living Faithfully Now* (Grand Rapids: Brazos, 2022).

On Thanks

Give thanks! Offering thanksgiving throughout the day is not necessarily an unusual act for a person of faith, but the psalms put a particular spin on it. A general thanksgiving for God's provision in terms of daily sustenance is no small matter, but thanksgiving in Psalms doesn't just sit there. These psalms live on the other side of lament.[24] As such, when we read these holy poems, we are molded in a specific way.

As discussed above, a lament cries out to God for help, deliverance, or security in an especially difficult situation. The theological background for the psalmists, then, is that God cares, hears, and can do something about the psalmist's pain, however defined. Unsurprisingly, in response to those laments, God answers: he helps and heals. Yet that is not where the story should end.

Thanksgiving may sound similar to praise psalms, and in many ways, it is. Distinct, though, is that thanksgiving is often the response of the psalmist to a particular moment of deliverance. The psalms once again move us, gently, subtly, and explicitly, to observe the pain *and* God's remedy. Once God's benevolent love is experienced, however, we shouldn't then go back to normal: it's not business as usual. These psalms call us to stop, individually and corporately, to proclaim the specific ways in which God has helped us in a time of trouble.

Recalling the Past

Memory is a funny thing today. At one time, I had scores of phone numbers saved in my brain, ready to punch the numbers when needed into a (yes, landline) phone for any possible emergency or perhaps a chat with my then fellow thirteen-year-olds. Now all I need is a few pushes on my smartphone. I don't need to recall important numbers quickly or confidently, but if I'm honest, this becomes a big problem when my bank or pharmacy asks me for my wife's phone number and my phone isn't close.

Suffice it to say, memory isn't prized today. That was quite different for the ancients, however. Depending on the specific time and cul-

24. Brueggemann, *Message of the Psalms*, 125.

ture, good memory could be an indicator of one's intellect, wisdom, or both, but most of us today just go to Google. The psalms stress the role of memory.[25] A particular group, the historical psalms, rehearse moments in Israel's history, but crucially, they provide more than a history lesson.[26] The repetition of the past serves the present: citing God's works brings to mind the marvelous wonders of the triune God.

In recalling that God has indeed delivered Israel from the Egyptians, for instance, the psalmist and the congregation stand at the ready, prepared to walk the next step in faith. This isn't a trite point. Take Psalm 105, for example. It starts with thanksgiving and calls the hearers to "remember the wonders that [the LORD] has done" (v. 5). These wonders begin with Abraham; the poem then moves the focus to Egypt. The ten mighty acts (plagues) are briefly described. The psalm concludes with Israel receiving the lands of nations "so that they would keep his statutes" (v. 45).

Similar yet different is the next poem: Psalm 106 recounts history, but with a focus on *disobedience*. "Our fathers in Egypt did not regard your wonders; / they did not remember the greatness of your loving-kindness. . . . Yet he saved them on account of his name" (vv. 7–8). The failings of Israel are put into relief with this psalm, only to make God's acts all the more astounding. "He remembered for them his covenant; / he had compassion according to the greatness of his loving-kindness" (v. 45). These adjacent psalms show that the historical can be recalled for different ends. Thanksgiving (Ps. 105) and lament (Ps. 106) are just two examples.

These historical psalms prompt us to recall God's acts within the world. While short memory may be the trend in our modern, technology-driven society, Psalms demonstrates the importance of remembrance. Knowing the story of God's mighty works molds us

25. Notably, memory is a trending topic in scholarship. What some scholars consider the role of memory isn't what I'm dealing with here. Cf. Maria-Sabina Draga Alexandru and Dragoş C. Manea, eds., *Religious Narratives in Contemporary Culture: Between Cultural Memory and Transmediality*, Studies in Religion and the Arts 17 (Leiden: Brill, 2021).

26. See further Vivian L. Johnson, *David in Distress: His Portrait through the Historical Psalms*, LHBOTS 505 (London: T&T Clark, 2009).

and prepares us for so much. We recall that Israel failed in specific and indeed significant ways, yet the Lord stayed true to his covenant; we can have confidence as we lament (cf. Ps. 106) or give thanks because of what he has done (cf. Ps. 105). In any case, knowing the story, as it were, isn't simply an issue of knowing the facts. Instead, these memories shine a light on the path as we walk with God.

On Natural Things

The psalms see life differently. For most of us, when we look around, we spot rocks, trees, and mountains and leave it at that. Perhaps we step back and have a moment of awe—that is, of course, if we take the time and opportunity to experience the natural world. When we open the book of Psalms, the picture becomes much clearer and livelier.

Rocks *praise*, rivers *clap*, and mountains *sing*. The natural world, better known as creation, brings forth praise to the living God, its Creator. While Scripture at large gives evidence of the significance of nature, no other biblical book does what Psalms does, certainly not as often. The poetry of Psalms helps move the reader into right understanding and right experience. Walking through life, we should be aware of the created order: birds, trees, rivers, stars, the whole lot. The point is not merely to become a "nature lover" or to uphold some political agenda.[27]

In reading Psalms, we observe the textual world, and from there the poetry performs. Labels like "animate" and "inanimate" lose their sharpness in these poems. We might be inclined to say that birds sing, but rivers and trees don't. In that very classification, we are helped by knowing that the cultural air we breathe is specific, if not peculiar. Our immediate thought on what creation is and does differs from the testimony in Psalms.

I must add, though, that terms like *anthropomorphism* won't do. To think that "rivers clap[ping] hands" is just a little figure of speech

---

27. For a careful and accessible discussion, see Sandra L. Richter, *Stewards of Eden: What Scripture Says about the Environment and Why It Matters* (Downers Grove, IL: IVP Academic, 2020).

misses the purpose of the poetry (cf. Ps. 98:8). Creation praises God. Steady and true, unprodded and unprovoked, creation praises.[28] Contrasted with humanity, creation becomes our teacher. We often need to be called, summoned, even shaken to praise the holy God. Like watching a sage grandmother who knows herself and her God deeply, a woman who can seamlessly move from forgiving someone to hosting another and praying for yet another, creation all around us shows us a long kind of obedience, a wisdom that reflects Wisdom. Thus, the poetry, its language and content, gives shape to our soul. We are moved by the fact that, first, we are not the only ones to be called "creation." Second, we can and should praise more often than we do. Third, we—along with trees, rivers, mountains, and more—are part of the choir that sings to the living God.

Conclusion

Psalms poetry is not merely for listening pleasure, and it doesn't exist to entertain. Nor does it prop up a cold, emotionless life of faith. The form of poetry at large brings us into contact with images that invite trust and display terror, distress, and pain most vividly. The poetry is felt. The forms of poetry, whether lament or praise, give structure and content to altogether normal rhythms of life. Psalms poetry is open, waiting for us to pick up and read. Read and pray; pray and sing. It's for the lonely individual and for the excited congregation. The seasons of the soul are described and displayed. The faithful reader today isn't meant to glance at this book to see how things once were. Rather, it's to show us primarily how things *are* and *will be*.

This chapter has been but an introduction. We've seen and heard the relationship of poetry to life, its shaping effect. Much of what's been presented will be exemplified in the readings in part 2. There

---

28. See, e.g., Ellen F. Davis, *Scripture, Culture, and Agriculture: An Agrarian Reading of the Bible* (Cambridge: Cambridge University Press, 2009); Richard Bauckham, *Bible and Ecology: Rediscovering the Community of Creation* (London: Darton, Longman & Todd, 2010); David Rensberger, "Ecological Use of the Psalms," in Brown, *Oxford Handbook of the Psalms*, 608–20.

we will look at the grandeur of specific poems, the granular beauty of lines, sounds, metaphors, and more. As one might expect, we will pay special attention to the ways the psalms whittle and mold us. Thus, we won't be concerned only with understanding the psalms, but also with imbibing them.

PART 2

Experiencing
the Restorative Power
of Poetry

— 5 —

Juxtaposition in Poetry

PSALM 1

What is the good life? Answers abound throughout the current moment: marketers, gurus, and so-called influencers all have a vision. As we open this book of poetry, the poems invite us to ponder what the good life is. Thankfully, its vision differs from what is on offer in this age of distraction. Psalm 1 specifically brings a theological view of human flourishing home through juxtaposition.

-------------------- **PSALM 1** --------------------

¹ Blessed is the man
  who walks not in the counsel of the wicked,
nor stands in the way of sinners,
  nor sits in the seat of scoffers;
² but his delight is in the instruction of the LORD,
  and on his instruction he meditates day and night.

³ He is like a tree
  planted by streams of water,
that yields its fruit in its season,

and its leaf does not wither.
In all that he does, he prospers.
⁴ The wicked are not so,
    but are like chaff that the wind drives away.

⁵ Therefore, the wicked will not stand in the judgment,
    nor sinners in the congregation of the righteous;
⁶ for the LORD knows the way of the righteous,
    but the way of the wicked will perish.

The first word grounds us. We find the description of one who is firmly set in a world swirling with difficulty. In reading the opening line of the poem, it is unfortunate that nearly every translation of this first word ("happy" or "blessed") has the potential to mislead. Suffice it to say, this poem has little to do with the ephemeral nature of what we typically label as happiness, nor does it necessarily speak to various physical attainments (blessings), though the psalm is not antithetical to them. By reading only the first word of the Psalter, we're reminded that poetry is a slow business. A quick glance or speed-reading won't suffice.

Beyond the initial word, the opening lines live in the negative. At first blush, this may seem to be an odd introduction. Why lead off with what *not* to do? In part, the reason is that the poet wants to lay the groundwork for what is all too easy and accessible. The psalm considers the most natural path its readers would walk. From there, the psalmist gives a poetic lecture on why that path is fruitless.

Each of the negative lines in verse 1 repeats. Like any good piece of music, repetition serves memory and meaning. Put differently, recurrence helps us know what to expect (at least broadly) when we approach the next line. In verse 1, repeated words ("not" and "in"), similar verbs ("walks," "stands," and "sits"), and nearly synonymous nouns ("wicked," "sinners," and "scoffers") all shape the lines and provide cohesion. Reading the poem, it would be wrong to conclude, "These lines are saying the same thing." It would be equally off course if one were to think, "Each line is saying something entirely different." The truth lies in the middle. Letting these lines simmer through careful repetition proves extraordinarily helpful.

The negative path leads first to the counsel of the wicked. The verb "walk" is often used to communicate affiliation and at times obedience and allegiance (1 Kings 18:21). Thus, the connection of "walk" with "counsel" is unsurprising in verse 1. The defining description for this poetic line appears with the noun "the wicked." This is most precisely where and with whom the blessed one should *not* be. Similar locales are "sinners" and "scoffers" in the next two lines. As stated above, these categories are not exactly the same, but the most noticeable distinction comes in the final line. The "scoffers" are ones who display their evil *with their mouths.* So whereas the first two, the "wicked" and "sinners," are reasonably clear descriptors, the final one leaves these three lines with the most refined image. The structure of the verse invites reflection on the life of the blessed one by imagining those who are not blessed.

A subtle, implicit move within the opening verse has to do with time. The pace by way of the verbs "walks," "stands," and "sits" slows from an amble to a comfortable recline. In a sense, the movement has stopped. No longer walking or standing, the poetry *sits.* The intersection of *sitting* and *scoffing* prompts reflection but is not easily reduced to one didactic point. In light of verse 1, of course, one could say, "Don't hang out with bad people," which is not entirely wrong, but the movement of the poem itself allows the images to wash over the reader. These verbal pictures intimate the ease and danger of receiving and participating in foolish counsel. The pace of the introductory lines puts rhythm in the mind and words in the mouth.

Once we reach verse 2, we realize that the opening verse is a purposeful preface for these two lines. The contrast ("but") between verses 1 and 2 is strong. In verse 2 it is "in the instruction of" that's repeated, but the lack of symmetry in the latter half of the verse does a lot of work for the poem. From the first line of verse 2, it is clear that the instruction comes from "the LORD." A key detail of the line is "delight" that the blessed one has in the Lord's instructions. With the word "delight," we most clearly enter the emotive world of poetry. This line challenges all who would associate obedience with drudgery. Delight opens our eyes to the world of desire and joy. Crucially, this delight is in contrast with the accessible and prevalent path of the wicked. As these lines come together, the reader is not called simply to take a different path; instead, the poem invites the joy of the reader to reside "in the instruction of the LORD." Juxtaposition between the first two verses plays a large role in developing the richness of "delight."

The second line of verse 2 colors our picture of what delight looks like. Unlike the simple verb "is" in the first line, the second line specifies that the blessed one "meditates" on the instruction of the Lord.[1] Once again, translations tend to lead to unproductive paths. Meditate conjures up a host of different images, but the more precise sense of the verb here has to do with speaking or muttering. In other words, the blessed ones will turn the instruction of the Lord over and over in their mind and mouth. The poetic connection of verse 2 demonstrates that delight has something to do with reflection; one is not in isolation from the other. Moreover, this *meditating* should be practiced "day and night."

The poetry hits us here. This is not a literal delimiting of the specific times when one should have delight, but the use of the temporal pair suggests continuous, repeated acts that are couched in delight. The poetry sets "delight" and "mediate" next to one another, opening up life in the everyday, during "day and night." By the end of verse 2, the whole person is awakened to life that brings to mind the instruction of the Lord.

The next verse moves us further into the world of the imagination. The agronomic life frames the image, making the selection of a "tree" most sensible (v. 3). Modern readers, however, may experience some latency in feeling the imagery. In any case, we need to be led to the agricultural comparison of the tree and the blessed one. The specifics of the tree, its genus and so on, prove irrelevant. It is as if the poet writes, "Think of a tree, the tree that first comes to your mind; whether it is oak, fig, or olive is immaterial." This tree is "planted by streams of water." The interrelation of "water" and "tree" is clear, regardless of one's knowledge of ecology: without the former, the latter does not live. Yet the poem has more in mind than just living.

---

1. The Hebrew text of the first line (v. 2) is a verbless clause. Translations typically supply the copula "is" (cf. ESV).

The next three lines of verse 3 make abundantly clear that *flourishing* is in view. First, the tree "yields its fruit." Thus, staying alive is not the telos of the image: the tree is meant to thrive. What is more, the fruit comes "in its season." Such a statement strikes most of us moderns as odd. At almost any time of year, we can walk into a grocery store and pick up fruit that is not at all in season in the region where we live. Oranges are flown in from around the world, and strawberries appear at peculiar times, but such is the modern economy.[2] Current food economics for the industrialized world are not analogous to the regionalized food supply of the ancient world. The little phrase "its season" brings us back to the nature of time and pace in the poem. The line presses the reader to consider not a tree that bears fruit *at all times*, but one that does so in its proper time. In other words, the tree is thriving in an ordered way, in accord with its design.

Through the poetic juxtaposition of imagery, our soul is shaped by expectation: timing, seasons, patience, and altogether slow (as opposed to instant) growth flood the mind from the force of the image (cf. John 15). The reader who takes delight and mediates on the instruction of the Lord should anticipate flourishing as a natural outcome. Nevertheless, the fruit is available only when it is ready. Like the blackberry bushes currently flowering in my back garden, the blessed tree or person may take months or years to produce fruit. The cycle of the thriving tree orders our heart for the seasons of life.

Second, the *flourishing tree* is given shape by its opposite: "Its leaf does not wither." During a period of drought or flood, the leaves maintain health. The poet gives no caveat to the verdant metaphor. On the other hand, *success* in "all that he does" (v. 3) has context, and its scope is *not limitless*. As mentioned, the tree bears fruit in its season, not in every season. Thus, one would be wrong to read quickly verse 3 as suggesting *success in all things* and think that nothing but green lights wait for us on the road of life. Yet by way of its imagery, the poetry has moved the vision of the reader to consider the way life can be. The psalmist is acutely aware of other paths of life (v. 1), but the flourishing tree trains the soul for a life of bearing fruit.

---

2. See further Norman Wirzba, *Food and Faith: A Theology of Eating*, 2nd ed. (Cambridge: Cambridge University Press, 2019), 71–109.

The following verse (v. 4) places certainty in the mind of the reader through juxtaposition: "the wicked" and "the blessed" are not the same. Just as the blessed one received lines of imagery, the wicked ones now show comparison. They are "like chaff." We again live in the agrarian world of the poem, even if we know nothing but the industrial age. The word "chaff" may make us pause, but the sense is quite plain. It constitutes the discarded husk "that the wind drives away" (v. 4). The poem does not offer the same detail for the chaff imagery as is given for the tree (v. 3). It seems that the tree, with its water, fruit, and unwavering leaves, gives layers to the invitation of blessing *in contrast with* the brief and flat presentation of the un-usable chaff.

Quite rare for Psalms poetry, verse 5 begins by teasing out the logic of the poem with an explicit syntactical connection: "There-fore," the line reads. We know that what follows has implications stemming from verse 4, yet the poem in verse 5 maintains clarity *and* ambiguity in drawing out the logic from the above verse. In terms of certainty, there is no mistaking that the reader should avoid the life of the "wicked" and the "sinner." Opacity creeps in with verse 5. For instance, what *exactly* does it mean that the "wicked will not stand in the judgment"? Is the implication that they cannot be pres-ent for judgment? The second line provides some clarity: "Sinners [will not stand] in the congregation of the righteous." Here it seems that they will not be able to experience life with the congregation. In any case, this is a reminder that separation is part and parcel of Psalms poetry.

The reality that the blessed flourish and the wicked cannot stand in judgment concludes in a simple but profound way: "the LORD knows" (v. 6). The last verse brings the poem to a close. This theo-logical crescendo, however, has an unexpected note. The first line of verse 6 brings transparency and encouragement to the righteous: the Lord knows *their way*.[3] The second line holds the symmetry of the first. The word "way" is repeated with the "wicked," but strikingly, the verb from the A line ("knows") is not. Instead, "the way of the

---

3. On this use of the participle "knows," see, e.g., Christo H. J. van der Merwe, Jacobus A. Naudé, and Jan H. Kroeze, *A Biblical Hebrew Reference Grammar*, 2nd ed. (London: Bloomsbury T&T Clark, 2017), §20.3.3.1.

wicked" serves as the subject for the last line of the poem; in so doing, it loads the last line with a sobering reminder: the way of the wicked "will perish." Again, juxtaposition does its work.

If we were to scan this poem and swiftly walk away with a prompt to read our Bible more, I suggest that the poetry of Psalm 1 would not have been heard. This psalm outlines the beauty of blessedness by highlighting the ease and destruction of paths before the reader. Thus, our poet brings us to improper ways and details their defunct nature. Yet the heart of the psalm invites the imagination into the agrarian world to see and experience the life of the blessed one. The road of the imagination is paved with delight and meditation. The life of one immersed in the instruction of the Lord flourishes and thrives. The wicked, however, find a different end as, ultimately, their way *perishes*.

The last line brings a weightiness to what could otherwise be a cheery psalm. The poem pronounces that life is not a game. The poetry draws a line between two groups: the wicked and the righteous. The move of the poetry is not that the righteous are so *because* they delight in the instruction of the Lord. The righteous are righteous: no further consideration is given to how they are so. As the righteous have the disposition of delight and the activity of meditation, the causality of righteousness is not underscored, but the habit of it is.

In sum, simply reading Scripture is not necessarily a mechanism that triggers all things to go right and well in one's life. The delight of the blessed one centers on God. The life of the righteous is sustained in a confidence that stems only from God and his word. The contrasting imagery throughout the poem highlights the ephemerality of the wicked and the security of the righteous. Juxtaposition throughout the psalm provides a warm welcome to the flourishing life.

— 6 —

Openness in Poetry

PSALM 3

No one knows a life without suffering. Waves of pain rush through the physical, emotional, and social fabric of life. Anguish is inescapable, though not all suffering is the same. Psalm 3 moves us into the heart of psalms poetry and the life of pain. With words like "enemies," "foes," "many," and more, this open poetry offers an invitation to read, pray, and even sing along with the psalmist.[1]

Picking up Psalm 3 and experiencing its poetry can both soothe and steady the soul. This happens in at least three ways. First, the psalm directs our eyes to the pain or suffering we are experiencing (or might experience). Crucially for many in the modern West, it needs to be clear here that the notion of the psalmist's circumstances being worse than our own simply will not suffice as a reason to ignore the psalm or our pain. The purpose of this particular lament is in no way predicated on a comparison of the psalmist and the reader. Second, the psalm moves us to place trust in the Lord *while* we are

---

1. A notable exception is the superscription: "A psalm of David, when he fled from Absalom his son."

experiencing pain. Third, the poem instructs the person of faith to cry out to God for help and deliverance. No self-talk or psychoanalyzing is suggested by the poem. The poetic words welcome the weathered soul into a home that is safe, warm, and well-stocked. The visitor, worn through with worry and pain, need only seek the host.

───────────── **PSALM 3** ─────────────

¹ O LORD, how many are my foes!
    Many are rising against me;
² many are saying of my life,
    "There is no salvation for him in God." *Selah*

³ But you, O LORD, are a shield about me,
    my glory, and the lifter of my head.
⁴ I call out with my voice to the LORD,
    and he answered me from his holy hill. *Selah*

⁵ I lay down and slept;
    I woke again, for the LORD sustains me.
⁶ I will not fear some ten thousand
    who have set themselves against me all around.

⁷ Arise, O LORD!
    Save me, O my God!
For you have struck all my enemies on the jaw;
    you have broken the teeth of the wicked.

⁸ Salvation belongs to the LORD;
    your blessing be on your people! *Selah*

The first line sets the scene. "O LORD" defines the poem. Put differently, the psalmist is not merely voicing frustration into the air; the poem is prayer. All that follows must be heard in light of that frame. The prayer nonetheless begins with nothing but trouble. The first two lines make especially clear that the enemies are many. The intensity increases in the second line with the notice that many "are rising against" the psalmist (v. 1).[2] Even so, the openness of the poem remains, for the text is still silent on what of kind of battle is in view.

2. In this chapter, as with others, I am using the versification of the English Bible.

The next verse puts the suffering in a *verbal* frame: the words of the enemies brittle the bones. The many are saying of his life, "There is no salvation for him in God" (v. 2). Thus, the enemies' speech has a theological edge. The poetry brings us pause. Is it true? Does any deliverance come from the living God? The question is not theoretical for the psalmist—or for the reader. Here the lines highlight the potential destruction of words; this realization pushes us to consider whether faith can fail in light of these words, intent on dismantling trust in God.

The next line (v. 3) reaches for an answer that resonates against the enemies' question. This answer comes wrapped in proclamation. The psalmist states how God has cared for him and, in so declaring, subverts the speech of the enemies. Instead of saying, "No, it is not true," the psalmist tells of God's kind protection. To outline that protection in Psalm 3, as is the custom in Psalms, imagery does the heavy lifting. The psalmist speaks directly to God: "But you, O LORD, are a shield" (v. 3). Living and experiencing the imagined world for the moment, we sense that no matter the arrow or sword, the psalmist remains safe. The final word of the first line clarifies the imagery. The shield is "about" or "surrounding" the psalmist. We picture in our mind safety that has no vulnerability. The rest of verse 3 names God as the psalmist's "glory" and "the lifter of [his] head." In response to the enemies' claim of an incapable (or unconcerned) God, the psalmist defies the misinformed by recalling who God is and what God has done in his own life.

Within just a few verses, this psalm heartens readers to recall life with God. The testimony of God's gracious care in times of need should not be left on the pages of the mind, dusty and unused. These former moments give witness to the present. God always has cared for us. God cares for us *now*. This interpretive move does not render God mechanistic (cf. Job's so-called friends), nor does it elicit specifics of what provision will look like in the present. In any case, the flow of the poetry shows a towering wave of adversity and a call for distrust in God's care, but in that tumult, the psalmist does not waver. Since the language of the poetry is open to us, I suggest that the psalm should likewise move us to hold fast.

As the poem continues, the lines stack one on the other to give more detail. Leaving the metaphorical language of "shield" and "lifting of the head," verse 4 testifies to answered prayer. Simply put, the psalmist calls out with his voice to the Lord, and "he answered . . . from his holy hill." These verses of trust give both imagination and description for times of suffering. Although pain comes in various forms, this psalm has already demonstrated that the Lord hears, cares, and offers protection in the darkest night. Prayer here is not palliative, nor is this poem evidence that speaking into the air is cathartic. The living God hears the prayers of the psalmist and responds.

Verse 4 alone gives structure to our faith. At times, prayer can be construed as rubbing the lamp for a divine genie to come and do one's bidding. On the other end of the spectrum, prayer could be regarded as meaningless: God, the great arbiter of the world's affairs, will do as he will do, and engagement with humanity through prayer is superfluous. This vision would see prayer at best as a perfunctory act of piety. Yet the psalm more than nudges us in a different direction. Surrounded by enemies who are unimpressed by the Lord, the psalmist recalls the Lord's personal protection, specifically through answered prayer. This is not simply an advertisement or bumper sticker declaring, "Prayer works!" Instead, the poem illustrates the return to God in deep struggles by helping us recall God's gracious care and protection in our past. We are thus welcomed into such remembrance by the poetic language of the psalm.

Verse 5 narrates the calmed response of the psalmist. He *laid down*, *slept*, and *woke*. This is not a disinterested or despondent mode of living. Theology vivifies the verse here. Though logical and syntactical connectors are few in psalms poetry, the final piece of verse 5 gives the explicit, theological reason for unwavering rest: "*for* the LORD sustains me."[3] Dependence on God defines the life of the psalmist before, during, and after suffering.

Recalling rest and sleep in moments of chaos seems odd. It would perhaps be more natural to belabor all the details of present difficulties, but these daily acts of sleeping and waking are theological testimony. The witness of the poetry reverberates in the modern moment.

3. The choice of *yiqtol* here in Hebrew is particularly noteworthy. There is no end in sight for the Lord's sustaining care in the life of the psalmist. See further Bruce K. Waltke and Michael P. O'Connor, *An Introduction to Biblical Hebrew Syntax* (Winona Lake, IN: Eisenbrauns, 1990), §31.3.e.

The business of sleep is booming. The reason, at least in part, is that we are restless creatures, stirred well into the night by glowing screens of distraction. We desperately try to numb our boredom. Our present moment provides significant economic opportunity. People of average income now feel compelled, perhaps even entitled, to purchase a bed that is tantamount to a down payment on a house—all on the promise of better sleep. Melatonin, a once unknown hormone to the average person, is now a billion-dollar dietary supplement industry that even promotes products in gummy form for children as young as three years old. All is not well. In response, this psalm, not providing a cure-all for insomnia, presses us to consider further our daily rhythms and specifically the nature of our trust. The psalmist knows that the Lord sustains; the question for us is clear: Do *we* know that?

The poem does not struggle to communicate the confidence of the psalmist. Hyperbole serves verse 6 as the psalmist evidences trust: "I will not fear some ten thousand." While the enemies doubt and indeed try to sow doubt in the psalmist that the Lord will deliver, the poetry comes full-throated to confess assurance in the Lord. This confidence is by no means baseless. As mentioned, personal testimony serves as an ongoing sign that speaks in the defense of the psalmist. The imagination of some "ten thousand" people not inducing fear should grab and place us high on a steady rock amid the wild, lapping waves of life.

Only after detailing the tumult and the false confidence of the enemies does the psalmist call on the Lord to respond. The plea is simple: "Arise, O Lord! / Save me, O my God" (v. 7). The two short lines go hand in hand. The petition for the Lord to arise is clear and vague all at once. The clarity appears in the verb itself: "arise" gives a physical posture of attentiveness and conveys being ready to act. Directed to the Lord, the call is of course metaphorical, but the purpose of the rising must wait for the second line: "Save me." These lines together help us hear in surround sound the simple yet profound plea for help.

The lament of Psalm 3 centers on these few words of petition in verse 7. That seemingly simple observation can go a long way in shaping the soul. While most of the lament thus far has shown the difficulties surrounding the psalmist and the way theological reflection serves to bolster faith, the actual appeal is short and unassuming. There is a time and place for lengthy, theologically laden language in prayer, but let us be refreshed as well as challenged that brevity is not a negative. Calling out for God's deliverance is an act of faith, and this act does not need to be nuanced or complicated. It is often said, "We live in a complex world," or "Life is so complicated"; indeed, *complex* and *complicated* are sufficient adjectives for the present, but that is not to eschew deep faith expressed by brief prayer. For those with faith in the living God, the petition in verse 7 encourages, reminds, and illustrates how faith, at once simple and deep, is voiced.

Similar to the conclusion of Psalm 1, the latter portion of Psalm 3 surprises or even repels the modern reader. The psalmist seamlessly slides from the short, robust petition to giving a reason why the Lord should answer his prayer. Moderns may bristle at giving a reason (that is, including a rationale, for which God should answer prayer), but I suspect it is the *content* of the reason that proves the most troublesome. The lines read, "For you have struck all my enemies on the jaw; / you have broken the teeth of the wicked."[4] I suggest that the imagery in verse 7 is intended to color how we view the Lord's protection. So however one might feel about the Lord breaking teeth and striking jaws, let it be in the front of the mind that the psalmist is underscoring the protective acts of God. As seen in the earlier imagery of the surrounding shield, the lament poem of Psalm 3 demonstrates throughout its lines that the Lord cares for and defends the psalmist.

The final lines of the poem (v. 8) join together "salvation" and "blessing." The latter is in reference not only to the psalmist, but also to the Lord's people in general. The closure signals that both deliverance and blessing belong to the Lord. Thus, amid struggles such as these battles with enemies, the poem grounds the lament and petition in the reality that care, concern, and protection are gifts from the Lord.

This lament shapes our soul before, during, or after a season of pain and struggle; through the openness of poetic language, the

---

4. Deciphering the sense of time in the grammatical form (*qatal*) in v. 7 is especially difficult. For discussion and analysis on the language and interpretive significance, see Stephen A. Geller, "The 'Precative Perfect' in Psalms and the Struggle of Faith," in *The Unfolding of Your Words Gives Light: Studies on Biblical Hebrew in Honor of George L. Klein*, ed. Ethan C. Jones (University Park, PA: Eisenbrauns, 2018), 3–13.

psalmist invites us into this dialogue of pain and trust. We recall from whom our help comes. While many today may try to numb themselves to reality through narcotics (prescription or otherwise) or the so-called bingeing on media, the psalm confronts us. The poetry pushes us to take stock of the actual pain or suffering we experience so that our vision is open and clear to our sorrow; yet we do not stay there. As with the poet of Psalm 3, we recall the Lord's past care and also plead for help and deliverance in the present. Trust is the soil of this kind of petition. We do not throw prayers at the wall to see what sticks, nor do we simply rail at the divine. Trust resides in the living God, knowing that he loves, cares, and is capable of responding to our cries for help. "Salvation belongs to the Lord"—that is good news for any day, but perhaps especially today.

— 7 —

Repetition in Poetry

PSALM 8

Repetition "might prompt a sense of frustration, boredom," or dissatisfaction, but we all know it "makes perfect."[1] Much to the interest of this book, "repetition . . . turns out to be one of the most significant tools a poet has."[2] Thus, when reading Scripture, it's wise to ask, What is the purpose of a line repeating within a poem? In this chapter, I'll show how repetition shapes one of the most memorable poems in all the Psalter—namely, Psalm 8—and in turn draw attention to how repetition shapes *us*.

The poem opens and closes with the same line: "O LORD, our Lord . . ."[3] Accordingly, this psalm "interrupts the sequence of prayers for salvation" in Psalms 3–7 "to say something very important about the God to whom the prayers are made: The LORD is the cosmic

---

1. Sarah Houghton-Walker, *Wordsworth's Poetry of Repetition: Romantic Recapitulation* (New York: Oxford University Press, 2023), 3.
2. Houghton-Walker, *Wordsworth's Poetry*, 6.
3. Recently, while I was visiting a lovely congregation in England, a member opened and closed their intercessory prayer with the first and last lines of Psalm 8. It was a moving and instructive time of prayer.

sovereign whose majesty is visible in the whole world."[4] The poem is structured by recurrence; as a whole, the psalm exhibits a "composition" that is "exceptionally harmonious."[5]

Reiteration of the first line in Psalm 8 serves as a boundary marker, leaving the beginning and end of the poem uniform. The lines tell the reader, "Here is a complete and coherent poem; read on!" Yet the contribution can be felt beyond its function as a mere border. Reaching the end of the poem and retelling the first line, we experience the poetry differently. The line is the same, to be sure, but the recurrence scaffolds the soul by prompting recall of all that preceded it, allowing the Holy Spirit to shape our lives with the knowledge gained and the emotions experienced throughout the poem. Within the symmetrical edges of the first and last lines, the poem makes use of paradox and plays with the limits of language. Let's turn now to Psalm 8 and engage the poem from start to finish.[6]

--------------------- **PSALM 8** ---------------------

[1] O Lord, our Lord,
    how majestic is your name in all the earth!
You have set your honor above the heavens.
  [2] Out of the mouth of babes and infants,
you have established strength for the sake of your foes,
    to silence the enemy and the avenger.

[3] When I look at your heavens, the work of your fingers,
    the moon and the stars, which you have established,
[4] what is man that you remember him,
    and the son of man that you come to care for him?

4. James Luther Mays, *Psalms*, Interpretation (Louisville: John Knox, 1994), 65.
5. Samuel Terrien, *The Psalms: Strophic Structure and Theological Commentary*, Eerdmans Critical Commentary (Grand Rapids: Eerdmans, 2003), 126.
6. To recall, this book is not attempting to tackle every issue of Psalms interpretation. Thus, the important and vast topic of Christology and Psalms receives little attention here, but not due to a lack of interest. For a thorough treatment of Psalms that takes on both exegesis and theology, see Hubert James Keener, *A Canonical Exegesis of the Eighth Psalm: YHWH's Maintenance of the Created Order through Divine Reversal*, JTISup 9 (Winona Lake, IN: Eisenbrauns, 2013). For a New Testament treatment, see Michael Goulder, "Psalm 8 and the Son of Man," *New Testament Studies* 48, no. 1 (2002): 18–29.

[5] Yet you have made him a little lower than the heavenly beings
   and crowned him with glory and honor.
[6] You have given him dominion over the works of your hands;
   everything you have set under his feet,
[7] all sheep and oxen,
   and also the beasts of the field,
[8] the birds of the heavens, and the fish of the sea,
   whatever crosses along the paths of the seas.

[9] O Lord, our Lord,
   how majestic is your name in all the earth!

As with so many psalms, the first line of verse 1 begins with God's revealed name: the "Lord." This simple observation grounds our thoughts and directs our minds toward the one about whom the psalmist speaks. In terms of its form, the poem is properly called a hymn. Typically, a hymn can move from talking *about* God to talking *to* God directly. Psalm 8, however, is the only hymn that's directed *to* the Lord in every line.[7]

The second phrase follows by indexing the relationship: this God is "our Lord."[8] That is to say, our God is our master, or as another psalm would have it, "We are his people / and the sheep of his pasture" (Ps. 100:3). In Psalm 8, it becomes clear that the one to whom the people pray is the one whom they follow. For those of us who take up Psalm 8 as poetic Scripture, we assume the same role: he is *our Lord*.

The poetry of the hymn begins to stretch our imagination with the following line: "How majestic is your name in all the earth." This line presses on the mind the import of God's name throughout the globe. The Lord's magnanimity levels the reader with the truth that it's his world, and he has set his "honor above the heavens."[9]

7. Mays, *Psalms*, 65. Other hymns of praise are Pss. 33, 47, 48, 65, 66, 67, 68, 76, 83, 87, 89, 96, 98, 99, 100, 103, 104, 105, 111, 112, 113, 114, 117, 135, 145, 146, 147, 148, 149, and 150. See Rolf A. Jacobson and Karl N. Jacobson, *Invitation to the Psalms: A Reader's Guide for Discovery and Engagement* (Grand Rapids: Baker Academic, 2013), 46.

8. Notably, the word "Lord" is distinct from the divine name "Lord." The former can also reference people's relationships, as in Gen. 18:12; 23:6; 2 Sam. 15:15 (cf. Pss. 2:4; 16:2).

9. On the textual difficulty of "set" (*tanâ*) in v. 1, see Susan Gillingham, *Psalms through the Centuries*, vol. 2, *A Reception History Commentary on Psalms 1–72*, Wiley Blackwell Bible Commentaries (Oxford: Wiley Blackwell, 2018), 73.

As stunning as that is, we can become momentarily vexed in what follows. The Lord has "established strength" in the most unusual of places: "the mouth of babes and infants"; somehow this is a source of "power" (v. 2).

Concerning these young ones, "the poet may have had in mind the physical weakness and at the same time the infantile force of innocence and trust."[10] At this point, the poetry is at the precipice of the rational; somehow the final two lines of verse 2 push even further: "For the sake of [the LORD's] foes," he has done this. God's work accomplishes its purpose: "to silence the enemy and the avenger"; this is an illustration of how poetry can expand the mind. For example, how does strength relate to infants and in some way silence adversaries? The poetry prompts the question but does not give a full answer. Nonetheless, the paradox of strength and weakness encourages us in the modern moment, when so many are actively and viciously vying for power throughout the world: we learn that brute strength will not succeed. This truth prepares us for the portrait of Jesus in the Gospels, both the incarnation and his ministry. In the kingdom of God, strength is paradoxical.

The poem moves to a new scene in verse 3. This section relates to the first two verses and propels praise and theological reflection. The objects the psalmist highlights are "your heavens, . . . the moon and the stars." The first receives elaboration: the heavens are "the work of [the LORD's] fingers." With this phrase, the reader has a vivid sense of the detailed craftmanship. Looking at the heavens, the psalmist does not witness anything but the theological. This is God's work, and that reality prompts worship, both from the psalmist and from ourselves.

Similarly, "the moon and the stars" receive amplification: they are what the Lord has "established" (v. 3). The language of establishing and founding goes together, especially with the Lord as agent (cf. Ps. 24:2). In Psalm 8, we see that he has founded strength and established the moon and stars (vv. 2–3). Taken together, we find a rich, warm, and powerful image of the Creator God. As the lines start to stack up within the poem, we begin to grasp our place in the world. We live in the anonymous first-person "I" of verse 3. Thus, the vast

10. Terrien, *Psalms*, 129.

heavens and the sizable moon and stars leave not only the psalmist but also us feeling small, perhaps even insignificant. It is no wonder that the next verse (v. 4) considers the question "What is man that you remember him?"[11] Surely, humans are not worthy enough to demand the attention of God, we're led to think. The Lord must indeed be too lofty for this kind of care and concern, right? The B line of the verse (v. 4) reinforces the wonder: "What is man . . . *that you come to care for him?*"

The structure of the psalm highlights the interrogatives. Susan Gillingham notes that while the psalm "begins and ends with praise to God in the heavens" (vv. 1, 9), God's interaction with humanity at the center of the poem stresses "the place of man on earth" (v. 4).[12] The questions resound in our imagination, especially for verse 4; it is as if the psalmist were awaiting an answer.[13] The question is not after a definition of humanity, but clarity on *why* the Lord remembers and visits.[14] For those of us distracted and bored with all that modern life affords us, this poetry grabs our attention and demands our steady devotion. To recall chapter 1 above, this poem is worth our effort in paying attention.

The poem doesn't move into a direct response to the question "What is man?" The following verse (v. 5) instead pivots so as to sketch out the complexity of the created order. "By a sudden change, the poet continues to develop his feel of wonder," Samuel Terrien notes.[15] While humanity may seem insignificant (v. 4), the Lord has "made him a little lower than the heavenly beings" (v. 5). The second line of verse 5 then stirs with specificity: "glory and honor" are given

11. A responsive and reflective reading is Madipoane J. Masenya (ngwan'a Mphahlele), "Black (Humanity) Is Beautiful! Reading Biko and Meditating on Psalm 8," *Theologia Viatorum* 38 (2014): 1–13.

12. Gillingham, *Psalms through the Centuries*, 72. The structure of the poem in relation to these questions is tighter and more obvious in Hebrew than in English because the same interrogative is used throughout (*mah*), which is translated "how" in vv. 1 and 9, but "what" in v. 4; cf. Dieter Böhler, *Psalmen 1–50*, HThKAT (Freiburg: Herder, 2021), 167.

13. Of interest, John Calvin finds that Ps. 8 speaks of creation, whereas the center of the psalm (vv. 4–5) has to do with Christ (see Gillingham, *Psalms through the Centuries*, 78).

14. Mays, *Psalms*, 67.

15. Terrien, *Psalms*, 130.

to humanity, or more specifically, the Lord crowns them. Thus, without ever using the exact words, the poem pictures humanity as kings and queens. We now see ourselves in a better light, Scripture's light. The result of rehearsing the psalm so far is a multifaceted picture of the Lord and creation, with special attention given to humanity.[16]

The psalmist teases out the interrelations of creation. The Lord has caused humanity to rule over the works of his hands (v. 6). Consequently, humans have the works of God as their domain. The specificity of the scope comes in the next line of verse 6: "Everything you have set under his feet." This verse signals that the world is under the Lord's direction and that, within it, humanity executes governance.

The stretch of verses 4–6 stresses that all is due to the Lord: he remembers, comes and cares for, makes less, crowns, causes to reign, and sets. The Lord is the subject of each line. The quick, clipped pace of the hymn gives the reader a rightly shaped vision for living: human beings are recipients of the Lord's gracious work. Therefore, as we have abundant opportunity to think that we are the engineers of our life, due in no small part to the messaging of modern media, this poetry humbles us. The glory, the rule, and the care of humanity find their source in the Lord alone. While there are dark moments in life and in the psalms, this poem bolsters the soul by showing creation's dependence on the Lord.

Everything under humanity's foot now gets spelled out. From birds to beasts, from fish to flocks, the poem specifies the stewardship of humanity.[17] The focus is certainly not on *how* humans should care, but more so on *what* humans should care for. The poem has moved us from the grand vision of the Lord's name throughout the earth to humanity being given glory and crown as well as the exercise of that rule over creation. The last word, however, is not about creatures, but the Creator.

As seen, the poet frames the psalm with the Lord's name and places humanity in the middle of that frame. The flow of the poem helps to "situate humankind in their fragility and greatness between

---

16. This is similar though notably distinct from Gen. 1–2.

17. For further study on animals in Ps. 8 and beyond, see Katharine Dell, "The Use of Animal Imagery in the Psalms and Wisdom Literature of Ancient Israel," *Scottish Journal of Theology* 53, no. 3 (2000): 275–91.

the majesty of God" and the animal kingdom.[18] What's more, we can readily hear "a symphony of delight upon the unfolding of the theology" from the first line of the psalm.[19] The poem is underwritten by the theology of God's dominion, "a hallmark of the Psalter," which is to say, God rules and reigns.[20] With repetition, this psalm has guided us to wonder and, in turn, worship the true and living God, the Creator, our King.

---

18. Terrien, *Psalms*, 126.
19. Terrien, *Psalms*, 126.
20. Mays, *Psalms*, 66. On the Lord's name in all the earth, Böhler reads this verse with Exod. 9:16 (*Psalmen 1–50*, 169), as he reads the whole of Ps. 8 against the early chapters of Exodus, with notable overlap in vocabulary.

— 8 —

Paradox in Poetry

PSALM 13

Feeling alone in a sea of people is an experience many of us have had. Songwriters and poets often explore this deep and paradoxical moment. As troubling as this emotional isolation is, Psalm 13 speaks to something more intense. The psalmist not only experiences loneliness, but also abandonment—notably, *divine* abandonment. This is one of the more complicated and distressing events in the book of Psalms. Before we try to explain the psalm away, let's be clear that the words of abandonment from the psalmist aren't merely perception. This prayer poem has something altogether rich and difficult for readers across the centuries. Psalm 13 presses on us the paradox of God as the problem and the solution.[1]

——————————— **PSALM 13** ———————————

[1] How long, O Lord—will you forget me forever?
How long will you hide your face from me?

---

1. We remember Augustine's wisdom that Scripture, notably Ps. 13, "adopts our human idiom." Augustine of Hippo, *Expositions of the Psalms: 1–32*, trans. Maria Boulding (Hyde Park, NY: New City, 2000), 173.

² How long will I take pain in my life,
     vexation in my heart daily?
How long will my enemy be over me?

³ Look! Answer me, O LORD, my God!
     Light up my eyes, lest I sleep the death,
⁴ Lest my enemy say, "I have prevailed over him!"
     My foes will shout, for I am shaken.

⁵ But in your steadfast love, I have trusted.
     Let my heart rejoice in your salvation!
⁶ Let me sing to the LORD,
     for he has dealt generously with me!

As with Psalm 8, Psalm 13 leverages repetition for its own ends. The particular purpose in this case is to direct the Lord's attention to the paradox of the psalmist's pain. The psalm opens with a direct, rhetorically laden question: "How long?" Like so many poems in Scripture, the words are spoken *to* the Lord, not merely *about* the Lord. Poetry and prayer blend together in the book of Psalms in an almost indistinct way. The pointed question to the Lord can take us aback. Some today don't feel comfortable in lamenting to God the way Psalm 13 does.² I suspect there are a few reasons why.

First, many are taught prayer by way of the Lord's Prayer (Matt. 6:9–13). This prayer, perhaps better named "The Disciple's Prayer," is significant in grounding disciples in a daily state of dependence on their heavenly Father. Yet the prayer is not intended to cover the entire scope of life. We should not expect that every situation in a pilgrim's life can be neatly tucked into this oft-recited Scripture.³ Second, I find it likely that the typical presentation of "the fear of the LORD" has something to do with our unease of saying Psalm 13 as our own. This might seem off topic, but it isn't. We typically hear "the fear of

---

2. This is even more so for a more specific category of lament—namely, imprecatory psalms. For some important work on this topic in relation to context, see David Tuesday Adamo, "The Imprecatory Psalms in African Context," in *Biblical Interpretation in African Perspective*, ed. David Tuesday Adamo (Lanham, MD: University Press of America, 2006); Solomon Olusola Ademiluka, "The Use of Imprecatory Psalms in African Context," *African Journal of Biblical Studies* 23 (2006): 53–62.

3. Though, notably, both Ps. 13 and the Lord's Prayer center on dependence.

the LORD" as meaning reverential awe (cf. Prov. 1:7).[4] This frequent gloss is good so far as it goes, but if respectful reverence—especially in the sense of politeness—is fundamental to faith, then this intense lament psalm has no place to land in the life of the church.[5] Third, many (though not all) consider it more appropriate to stuff frustration, angst, and uncertainty deep down, instead of expressing these unsettling feelings. Even in an age of supposed authenticity, one might be more comfortable in posting a complaint about life on social media than lamenting to God about the given situation.

Poetry carries potential. This mode of language can hold tensions in a way that most of us are unaccustomed to. For instance, students I know become twisted up over the first two lines of verse 1. "How can this be so?" they ask. Perhaps the psalmist has misunderstood God, they suggest. They consider the possibility that God has changed rather dramatically once one turns to the Gospel of Matthew. Such theological reflection is dimly lit and in need of Scripture's light, especially with the ever-lurking shadow of Marcion.

Repetition of the question "How long?" sharpens the emotional edge of the prayer. The psalmist won't let go. We see something of the substance of faith. By this, recurrence of the psalmist's question instructs the reader. The first line resounds with a charge: "Will you forget me forever?" This accusation toggles between passive and active. While forgetting is more a passive act, the psalmist seems to be saying that the Lord is intentionally *not remembering*.[6] The next line ramps up the intensity. The psalmist claims that the Lord is hiding his face from him. The question is "How long?" The poetry here stacks the lines so that the emotion roars and leaves an echo reverberating in a seemingly empty sky. There is no answer, at least not yet.

The most concrete question comes last. The psalmist asks, "How long will my enemy be over me?" These words detail the present

4. "The fear of the LORD" (e.g., Ps. 19:9) may well entail reverential awe, but it is certainly more than that (e.g., Eccles. 12:13). For a biblical and theological treatment, see Tremper Longman III, *The Fear of the Lord Is Wisdom: A Theological Introduction to Wisdom in Israel* (Grand Rapids: Baker Academic, 2017).

5. This is not to imply that the psalm is irreverent.

6. For an insightful discussion of remembering in the Psalter, see Megan Daffern, "The Semantic Field of 'Remembering' in the Psalms," *JSOT* 41 (2016): 79–97.

reality of the psalmist and, at the same time, claim that the Lord
has neither remembered nor shown his presence through deliverance. In other words, the victorious enemy speaks to the reality that
the Lord has not protected the psalmist. The poem, as expected, is
quite theological.

Despite the discomfort that some of us may have in praying this
psalm to God, I suggest that the tension is intentional on the part of
the poet. The generalized language of suffering and enemy could fit
different lives at different times. Furthermore, when we take a step
back and realize that we are reading this prayer in Scripture, our eyes
see more clearly how to treat this poem. God is not averse to hearing
prayers that lead off with "How long . . . ?" The psalm testifies that
God does not balk at the more specific and seemingly inappropriate "Will you forget me forever?" and "Will you hide your face?"
Crucially, these questions are layered with theology; they speak in
the language of trust, without using the word.[7] The psalmist finds
that the world is the Lord's, and, as such, his own life is the Lord's
concern.

The lament demonstrates an expectation that God will hear. As
noted before, this does not envision a mechanistic view of faith; instead, it is a fully sobered look at suffering that holds tightly to the
patience, the care, and the love of God. Put differently, the first two
lines of the poem take as a starting point that God *remembers* and
shows his face to the psalmist. The problem is that the psalmist's
circumstances are causing him to perceive the opposite: the Lord has
forgotten and has *hidden his face* from the psalmist. Nonetheless—
and this is a crucial point for modern readers—faith is not thrown
out on account of the situation. In fact, the suffering plunges the
psalmist deeper into the waters of trust.

The psalmist moves from lament to plea with little notice. After
issuing four "How long?" questions, the psalmist calls on the Lord
for help. Both lines of verse 3 are framed in oracular metaphor. The
psalmist calls for the Lord to look. Seemingly, once the psalmist has
caught the attention of the Lord, the expectation is that the Lord
will "answer" (v. 3a).

---

7. Yet the explicit language of trust does appear in v. 5.

The next line, as usual, gets more precise.[8] The psalmist asks the
Lord to "light up [his] eyes!" (v. 3b). "Light" often settles in close
with "salvation" in Scripture.[9] The poetic imagery prompts us to
feel the plea and not just understand it. The psalmist wants to *see*.
The phrasing here is multivalent. Certainly, the first sense leveraged
by the poetic plea is the physical life of the psalmist (as the next
phrase makes clear). The metaphorical language may also extend to
mean that the psalmist will see life as well as God more clearly. This
connection comes from the opening two lines. The present situation
shows the Lord's face as *hidden*. If God heeds the psalmist's plea,
then God's presence will be *seen* (at least in part).

Laments give us the language of faith. The language helps us
navigate life with God by seeing that God is not waiting to do our
bidding, nor is he so distanced and unconcerned that we should not
call out for him. In fact, the psalmist specifies reasons why the Lord
should "light up" the psalmist's eyes. These reasons serve to ground
the prayer and instruct the reader as well. The reasoning is general
but substantive: the psalmist will "sleep the death" (v. 3b). Under-
neath this reasoning is the simple truth that life is good.[10] This is not
to minimize the role of the Fall or to shortchange the significance
of the age to come, but rather to challenge the view that the present
physical life is not substantially good or that we are merely in some
waiting room before the coming age.[11]

Death entails more than the absence of life. The concern of the
psalmist centers on the boasting and rejoicing of the enemy at his
death. At stake would be something similar to Psalm 3: perhaps the
Lord isn't actually God. Maybe God doesn't care much for the psalmist *or* God is incapable of protecting him. In any case, the psalmist's

8. See further David J. A. Clines, "The Parallelism of Greater Precision: Notes
from Isaiah 40 for a Theory of Hebrew Poetry," in *Directions in Biblical Hebrew
Poetry*, ed. Elaine R. Follis, JSOTSup 40 (Sheffield: JSOT Press, 1987), 77–100.
9. See Isa. 2, 5, and 42.
10. The Old Testament frequently promotes the goodness of life. See Brent A.
Strawn, ed., *The Bible and the Pursuit of Happiness: What the Old and New Testaments Teach Us about the Good Life* (Oxford: Oxford University Press, 2012), 3–136.
11. A constant thorn in the side for the waiting-room view of this life can be seen in
the writings of N. T. Wright; see, e.g., Wright, *Surprised by Hope: Rethinking Heaven,
the Resurrection, and the Mission of the Church* (New York: HarperOne, 2008).

ensuing death would be testimony to the strength of his enemy over against God himself. As often in Psalms, a poetic line or two has the ability to compress matters that are theologically rich and deep. The final verses of the poem challenge interpreters. Readers aren't quite sure how to square verse 5 with the preceding lament and plea. Perhaps movement from the plea to the expression of trust is a temporal shift. The psalmist may be chronologically on the other side of pain by verse 5. In other words, he *has experienced* the salvation of the Lord. It is entirely reasonable, however, that the psalmist speaks these lines of trust *in the midst of* the suffering and lament.[12] In any case, the poetry proves the delimitation of these choices to be inconsequential. The stacking of lines, the absence of logical and temporal connectors, and the compressed syntax of poetry in general make verse 5 confounding and illuminating. The bewilderment has been noted already in the inability to discern the precise temporal relation of verse 5 to verses 1–4. The illumination comes in the interrelation of trust, praise, and lament. These elements, perhaps shocking to some moderns, provide a natural shape to the soul of the reader. Trust and lament, paradoxically, go together.

Trust is specified in Psalm 13. The psalmist anchors it explicitly "in [the] steadfast love" of the Lord.[13] This phrase "steadfast love" (*ḥesed*) has proved difficult to render.[14] The exact nuance can be difficult to discern in Hebrew and even more troublesome in translation. Nonetheless, the psalmist rests with confidence in the Lord's "steadfast love." There is a steady faithfulness of the Lord, as opposed to the mist-like love of humanity. Psalmists throughout the Psalter lean on and wrestle with God's steadfast love: at times, as in Psalm 13,

12. I tend to think that, in this psalm, trust is being expressed during the time of the suffering. The grammar and syntax support this idea. The first line, e.g., reads, "I trust" (*qatal*), and the second, "I will rejoice" (*yiqtol*). Certainly, the verbal system in Hebrew poetry does not play out systematically, but these lines seem to read just fine as evidence of present trust and future praise, thereby highlighting the confidence in the Lord for future deliverance.

13. Notably, there is the subject pronoun "I" (*'ānî*) leading the line. The pronoun is syntactically unnecessary (already in *bāṭaḥtî*) and specifies a first-person singular subject. Thus, the pronoun speaks to some type of pragmatic focus.

14. Carsten Ziegert, "What Is חֶסֶד [*ḥesed*]? A Frame-Semantic Approach," *JSOT* 44 (2020): 711–32.

they rest in it; other times, as in Psalm 85, they plead with God to show them steadfast love.

The God of steadfast love is also called "my God" (v. 3). Given the circumstances, the adjective "my" almost unsettles us. The Lord is the one who saw the affliction of the Israelites and heard their cries (Exod. 3:7), and now the psalmist asks, "How long, O Lord—will you forget me forever? / How long will you hide your face from me?" Invoking this covenant name, "Lord," with "my God" feels almost wrong, given the psalmist's lot, for where is this God of deliverance who sees and hears? To appeal to the name of God reads as if the psalmist is relying on the character of God in a situation in which the psalmist isn't experiencing the Lord's protection: it's a petition based on God himself instead of present circumstances.[15]

The next two lines fire the imagination as to how "steadfast love" operates in the life of the psalmist. This *love* surely has something to do with "salvation," for the psalmist implores, "Let my heart rejoice in *your salvation*" (v. 5). The Lord's steady faithfulness speaks to his strength and care to deliver the psalmist. The poem concludes in verse 6 with the psalmist wanting to "sing to the Lord, / for he has dealt generously with me!"[16] The final phrase seems to be framed in gentleness, perhaps recalling the image of a nursing mother (cf. 1 Sam. 1:23). The quick succession of lines has moved from lament to plea, from plea to trust, and finally from trust to praise.

This psalm witnesses pain and plea. Poetry's paradox shapes the soul first by drawing attention to the harsh realities of life. The edged descriptions are not dulled in the psalmist's prayer to the living God. In fact, the edges are sharpened since they are directed *to* the Lord, for the psalmist sees that the Lord has a part in his experience of pain. If the Lord would remember and show his face, then the situation would not be as it is (cf. Ps. 13:1). This is no mere complaint or emotional venting. The psalmist, amid all the pain, pleads with the Lord to "look" and to "light up [his] eyes" (v. 3). If the Lord does not do so, then all is lost (vv. 3–4). Despite the seriousness of the

15. I thank Sarah Haynes for several observations in this paragraph.
16. The verb "sing" is marked as a cohortative, typically as permissive or request: "Let me sing!"

situation, hope resounds (v. 5). Not only that: the psalmist declares future singing and praising to the Lord (vv. 5–6), in contradistinction to the enemies, who rejoice in the psalmist's defeat (v. 4).

As individuals and communities, this psalm instructs us—mind, body, and soul—to have no shame in being in desperate need of God's help. The tone and words need not be subdued when praying for God to upend, overturn, or rectify pain, whatever its particular frame. Through it all, trust is necessary. It is essential for us to trust that God can hear, care for, and speak to our suffering. When the difficulties come (and they will), we need not run to media to numb our mind, or gorge ourselves so as to forget, or obsessively work out in order to build self-esteem. Instead, we plead with God for help and deliverance. This poem takes us to the dark cellar of the soul: we feel the pain as we read and listen to the poetry. Nevertheless, lament is not the final word; praise triumphs.

— 9 —

Metaphor in Poetry

PSALM 42

Longing is a curious word. We don't use it too often. When we do, it usually conjures up ideas of being lovesick, with miles separating us from our significant others. Longing and all its emotional entailments become associated with this psalm.[1] The upshot is highlighting affections for God; the downside, which is significant, is that longing tends to miss the freight of the biblical imagery. The psalmist opens the poem in a cry of desperation, but not with any romantic sensibility. Thus, the reader who begins the poem while imagining the longing of two lovers is altogether on the wrong path.

Reading metaphors in Psalms can be difficult. Time, language, and culture separate us; yet we are not at a loss. Many tools have been developed in recent decades to account for the distance between us and Scripture. One essential though underutilized tool in understanding and imbibing the imagery of poetry, as noted above in chapter 3, is *patience*. It may sound entirely trite, but patience with Scripture's metaphors offers much to readers. At first blush, the contribution

1. See, e.g., Ps. 42 in NRSVue: "As a deer longs for flowing streams . . ."

of patience is a clearer understanding of the language of the Bible. Beyond that, a deeper work is stirring under the surface. Being patient with words simultaneously shapes our soul. In the moment of quick fixes, life hacks, and microwave everything, we as human beings need constant reminders to have an ambling pace. So rather than speed-reading or quickly getting to the point of the poem, let's open Psalm 42 and be instructed by its imagery.

PSALM 42

To the leader. A Maskil of the Korahites.

[1] As a deer pants for streams of water,
    so my soul pants for you, O God.
[2] My soul thirsts for God,
    for the living God.
When will I come and appear before
    the face of God?
[3] My tears have been my food
    day and night,
while people say to me continually,
    "Where is your God?"
[4] These things I remember,
    as I pour out my soul:
how I went with the throng
    and led them in procession to the house of God,
with glad shouts and songs of thanksgiving,
    a multitude keeping festival.

[5] Why are you downcast, O my soul,
    and why are you in turmoil?
Hope in God; for I shall again praise him,
    my help [6] and my God.

My soul is downcast within me;
    therefore, I remember you
from the land of Jordan and of Hermon,
    from Mount Mizar.
[7] Deep calls to deep
    at the thunder of your cataracts;

all your waves and your billows
    have gone over me.
⁸ By day the LORD commands his steadfast love,
    and at night his song is with me,
    a prayer to the God of my life.

⁹ I say to God, my rock,
    "Why have you forgotten me?
Why must I walk about mourning
    because the enemy oppresses me?"
¹⁰ As with a deadly wound in my bones,
    my adversaries taunt me,
while they say to me continually,
    "Where is your God?"

¹¹ Why are you downcast, O my soul,
    and why are you in turmoil?
Hope in God; for I still will praise him,
    my help and my God.

The first phrase of the poem compares the psalmist's soul with an animal: "as a deer pants" (v. 1). Reading the line, our imagination opens to a world of possibilities. For instance, what is the deer panting for? What is the purpose of the comparison? Where is the imagery meant to take us? Whatever the answer, the comparison to the deer reminds us that Scripture is native to the natural world. The imagery, however, does not necessitate us digging around in books or dirt in order to understand the many details and nuances of the animal. The rest of the line sets the boundary for how the imagery might teach the reader.

The "streams of water" entice the deer to pant. It is common knowledge that animals require water to live. Certainly, the quantity needed differs among the animal kingdom, but water is requisite. From that simple fact, our minds can start to wonder what might be unfolding from the comparison. Desperation likely moves to the front of our minds. If something of necessity, say water, is at a distance, then distress is ever-present. For the deer, life is found in the streams of water. That awareness of the imagery's edge propels us forward to find the contribution of the comparison.

The psalmist's soul parallels the deer: both pant. The key distinction lies in the object. The phrase that helps advance the lines is "for you" (v. 1). By this, we know that the psalmist is not speaking *about* God but rather is speaking *to* God. The stacking of lines shows that "God" and "streams of water" correspond. The force of this observation is not that God is like water at some general level. Rather, the relation of water to the deer frames the relation of God to the psalmist. That is to say, necessity and desperation are prominent notes. The reason for the distance between the psalmist and the Lord remains unclear at this point, but the darkness of desperation is palpable.

The second verse awakens the imagination as well as reiterates the imagery. The psalmist says his "soul [life] thirsts for . . . God." The metaphorical language of thirsting finds concrete expression elsewhere in the Old Testament. For instance, the Israelites, after the exodus from Egypt, "thirsted for water" (Exod. 17:3). They immediately "complained against Moses." In our psalm, the expression of desperation is not actually for water, but for God. The imagery links with the final phrase of the line, "the living God" (v. 2). Coming from the first verse, we picture living, or flowing, streams of water. No stagnant cesspool is envisioned. The imagery of the aquatic flow leads us to consider the psalmist's perception of God. Like the water, God is the source of life. This vision of God brings emotion and clarity to the table. God is where life is found; it is good, therefore, to be in urgent need of him.

The next line in verse 2 puts the imagery as a straightforward question: "When will I come and appear before the face of God?" The question is underwritten by the notion that if the psalmist is in the presence of God, then his life will be sustained. Perhaps in various ways we could say, "The psalmist *will live*." This simple question of *when* reminds us, in our present age of distraction, who God is. Of all the places, people, and things the psalmist could have turned his eyes to, God is the one in whom life flourishes (v. 1). These initial verses instruct us on our dependency and so prepare our soul for future moments of need.

Anguish pervades in the following line (v. 3). Water imagery stays as the psalmist moves to lament. Yet the metaphorical language becomes mixed as the psalmist's "tears" have become "food [bread]."

Water and food coalesce in a peculiar way. Underscoring the intense sorrow, the poetry adds "day and night." In the economy of words, this addition should not be missed. Markers of time and logical connectors are not necessary in poetry due to its appreciation for openness, ambiguity, and concise measure. These word choices forcefully increase the intensity of the poem.

The prompt for the psalmist's grief is verbal. Nameless and bold, some are saying to the psalmist "continually [all the day long], 'Where is your God?'" (v. 3). Throughout the Psalter, the words of others are pointed and violent. The sharpness of their speech presses against the psalmist's throat, perhaps forcing him to concur, at least in part: Indeed, "Where is [my] God?" The psalmist knows God to be life, but the flowing streams of the divine are at a distance.

Realities trigger memories. Such a truth cuts both ways. For the psalmist, distance between himself and the living God floods the mind with memories of walking "to the house of God" (v. 4). This walking would be full of "glad shouts and songs of thanksgiving" (v. 4). The imagination brings the taste of joy back to the psalmist's mouth, yet sight is not lost of the present pain. The psalmist asks, "Why are you downcast, O my soul, / and why are you in turmoil?" (v. 5). Pain, desperation, and questions of God's presence are swirling. Nevertheless, remembrance of joy and thanksgiving stirs the psalmist to reconsider. The present situation is not meaningless, but sorrow does not define the psalmist either. Here we're reminded not to dismiss or overlook various pains in life yet, at the same time, not to conflate our pain with our person.

The psalmist says to himself, "*Hope* in God!" (v. 5). Far from being self-talk or a call to pull himself up by his bootstraps, this charge draws on the truth that God is "the living God" (v. 2). There is a fine, nearly indistinguishable line between "hope" and "wait" in the Old Testament. For instance, the prophet Samuel tells Saul to go down to Gilgal and "for seven days *wait* till I come" (1 Sam. 10:8). In both the Samuel text and the psalm, this means a steady waiting. As for 1 Samuel, King Saul did not obey the prophet's words. The psalmist, however, takes to heart waiting and hoping for God (Ps. 42:5).

The vision of the psalmist is clear. He waits and hopes with a proper confidence that he will yet give thanks to God: deliverance is in the presence of his God (v. 5)! So much is left unsaid in this line. For example, how does the psalmist come to this kind of confidence? The answer partly lies in the next few lines. The psalmist reflects on the reason for the downcast state of his soul (v. 6). His words plant his pain in the memory of the reader: sorrow, desperation, and pain. Once again, in an unexpected use of a logical connector, the psalmist says, "*Therefore*, I remember you" (v. 6)! This movement from line to line scaffolds our soul so that God can begin to work on us. In a state of despondency, we can recall the living God, just as the psalmist does.

The poetry never chastises a downcast spirit, as if it were inherently wrong. In fact, the situation detailed in verse 3 seems to show a spirit less than joyful as a normal human experience. Already we have followed the movement of the psalmist, rehearsing the cutting speech of others and, in turn, remembering the act of worship and thanksgiving extended by the community (v. 4). Here in verse 6, however, the despondent psalmist recalls not activities of faith but God himself! The poetry thereby instructs us to do the same.

We return anew to the words "day" and "night" (v. 8). Our previous encounter involved the psalmist's tears being his food. Now the Lord commands his steadfast love *daily* (v. 8). In remembering God (v. 6), the psalmist has awakened to the fact that God ushers forth his own steady love. The full import of the Lord's love remains open for the moment. Nevertheless, our hearts are trained to grasp that God himself commands his love to human creatures. In a grief-laden psalm, the poetry reminds us of the steady acts of the living God. When our prayers seem to be stopping at the ceiling, the theological truth of the Lord's loving-kindness opens our imagination to what life is really like.

Poetry does not move in a sequential fashion, and the following verse (v. 9) serves as a case in point. While we leave what seems to be an almost happy tone of loving-kindness, prayer, and song, we move without warning into darkness. The first line of verse 9 tethers the psalm to trust. "I say to God, my rock," the line reads. In most cases, God as rock speaks to the protective and sure care that the Lord offers. It's an image of confidence. This use of the image makes good sense in light of the previous notes of God's daily acts (v. 8).

The remainder of the first line (v. 9) raises a question (cf. Ps. 13): "Why have you forgotten me?" The question, seemingly irreverent and inappropriate, comes from knowledge and trust in the Lord. As before, many a modern reader would be uncomfortable praying such a prayer. This psalm nonetheless rearranges our modern mental furniture so that we sit comfortably in the room with assurance *and* inquiry. In fact, it's *because* the psalmist trusts the Lord that he can ask these kinds of questions.

The psalmist pushes forward with his second question: "Why must I walk about mourning?" (v. 9). The imagery reminds us that salvation and deliverance are often represented by light, whereas danger, confusion, and need in general can be marked by darkness (cf. Pss. 35:6; 139:11). The undercurrent in the psalmist's questioning is that the Lord can manage events so that the psalmist does not walk in darkness any longer. The latter half of verse 9 puts darkness into concrete expression: the oppression of "the enemy." This line transitions the poem back to the straightforward description of the enemies. The line is a nearly exact repetition of verse 3. A key difference, however, lies in the beginning of verse 10: "with a deadly wound in my bones." The psalmist, speaking metaphorically, helps conjure up intense emotions, resulting in both understanding and sympathy. Put differently, this is no mere flesh wound: the deep and devastating blow has almost done in the psalmist.

We return to the tangible. This deadly wound is sourced from the enemies taunting the psalmist (v. 10). Now we see, with some repetition of verse 3, that *words* are the cause: the taunt is verbal. They question the psalmist: "Where is your God?" Once again, their derision is not without reason. The psalmist, who has been eating tears and walking in darkness (to name but two images), desperately wants to be in the presence of God (vv. 1–2). But thus far there has been no answer, even though the psalmist knows that the Lord commands his loving-kindness on a daily basis (v. 8). These questions to God lead again to questions of the psalmist. We hear the refrain: "Why are you downcast, O my soul, / and why are you in turmoil?" (v. 11). Three recurring interrogatives serve as a transition to the final line.

The psalm ends on a note that is not novel: "Hope in God!" (v. 11). This *waiting* or *hoping* shows resolve that is robust. This is no mere rehearsing of hope in a happy-go-lucky moment: pain, darkness, and taunt are all around. The call and the response grow in the soil of trust. This is most evident in the following phrase: "[Yet] I still will praise him." There is praise in the future but pain in the present. The Lord is the psalmist's Savior and God (v. 11). This proclamation finds no surprise since the psalm begins in a desperate plea for the presence of the living God.

In sum, we have seen through the poetry of the psalm, specifically with its imagery, the intensity and the distress of a life of faith. Ease of circumstances does not define the life of those who love God. Yet in pressurized moments, the images of Psalm 42 awaken us to life with God. Questions are not swatted away as inappropriate; yet it is the memory of who God is (v. 6) and what worship is like (vv. 4–5) that draw us to the testimony of God's love. In darkness and in the scoffing of those who do not love God, we remember with mind, body, and soul that the Lord is the living God. Our soul pants and thirsts for him (vv. 1–2).

– 10 –

Ambiguity in Poetry

PSALM 62

Ambiguity can frustrate. Having a conversation with someone who's speaking in vague terms or listening to a lecture that's unclear can leave us exasperated. The matter is different in poetry, which invites ambiguity, but not for the purpose of irritation. Ambiguity in poetry often prompts further reflection on the words, having us turn the language over and over in our minds. In Psalm 62, ambiguity pervades its structure and specific features, such as repetition and metaphor.[1] Wrestling with its ambiguity makes the text enjoyable and edifying, as the lines become lodged in the mind.[2] In a season of angst, we need to listen to this biblical poetry and be encouraged, be set aright.

As we read Psalm 62, two realities shine through. First is the pressure of life, and second is God himself. Psalm 62 allows us to enter a scene that is thousands of years past, but one that feels as fresh as

1. See also John Goldingay, *Psalms*, Baker Commentary on the Old Testament Wisdom and Psalms (Grand Rapids: Baker Academic, 2007), 2:245.
2. On memory and form, see Sean Burt, "'Your Torah Is My Delight': Repetition and the Poetics of Immanence in Psalm 119," *Journal of Biblical Literature* 137 (2018): 685–700.

today. The struggle, the vexation, the turmoil of life—all this is nothing new. This psalm has several addressees: the attackers, the faithful listeners, and God himself.[3] Yet in all of this, the poem centers on but one topic throughout: "trust" (named in v. 8).[4]

───────────── **PSALM 62** ─────────────

[1] For God alone my soul waits in silence;
        from him comes my salvation.
[2] He alone is my rock and my salvation,
        my fortress; I shall not be greatly shaken.

[3] How long will you assail a person,
        will you batter your victim, all of you,
        as you would a leaning wall, a tottering fence?
[4] Their only plan is to bring down a person of prominence.
        They take pleasure in falsehood;
they bless with their mouths,
        but inwardly they curse. *Selah*

[5] For God alone be silent, O my soul,
        for my hope is from him.
[6] He alone is my rock and my salvation,
        my fortress; I shall not be shaken.
[7] On God rests my deliverance and my honor;
        my mighty rock, my refuge is in God.

[8] Trust in him at all times, O people;
        pour out your heart before him;
        God is a refuge for us. *Selah*

3. We may well include the psalmist himself here too. For instance, Phil Botha notes that the psalmist addresses himself in vv. 5–7. "Psalm 62: Prayer, Accusation, Declaration of Innocence, Self-Motivation, Sermon, or All of These?," *Acta Theologica* 38 (2018): 34. As such, there would be a shift between vv. 5–7, where the psalmist is speaking to his own soul, and v. 8, where the psalmist is speaking to others. This perhaps intimates that the psalmist needs to reassure himself to trust in God before moving on to others. I thank Micah Barksdale for this observation.
4. I do not deal in detail with a particular genre of this psalm; the father of form criticism himself, Hermann Gunkel, notably called Ps. 62 a "special type." Thus, Erich Zenger is certainly on the right foot to focus on the particulars of the psalm, rather than broad similarities with other psalms. See Frank Lothar Hossfeld and Erich Zenger, *Psalms 2: A Commentary on Psalms 51–100*, trans. Linda M. Maloney, Hermeneia (Minneapolis: Fortress, 2005), 112–13.

⁹ Humans are but a breath;
  mortals are a delusion;
in the balances they go up;
  they are together lighter than a breath.
¹⁰ Put no confidence in extortion,
  and set no vain hopes on robbery;
  if riches increase, do not set your heart on them.

¹¹ Once God has spoken;
  twice have I heard this:
that power belongs to God,
  ¹² and steadfast love belongs to you, O Lord.
For you repay to all
  according to their work.

Discerning how the theme of trust develops throughout the poem is difficult. Many moments give us pause and make us ask, What exactly does this line mean?⁵ Ambiguity dwells throughout the poem. The flow of the psalm is in two parts: verses 1–8 and verses 9–12. Throughout, however, the psalm is filled with repeated words that are often lost in translation. A key word for reading this poem is "surely," perhaps better known from Psalm 23: "*Surely*, goodness and mercy will follow me" (v. 6). This word appears throughout Psalm 62 and sharpens the point.⁶ That said, within Psalm 62 the term highlights exclusion and is typically translated "only" or "alone." Thus, the poem stresses it is God *alone* and no other who the psalmist trusts.

This note of exclusion brings focus from the beginning. The psalmist's soul is in silence, and this silence holds the pressure of poetry.⁷ What does it mean to be silent?⁸ Is this a silent meditation? Is it a

5. On ambiguity being a significant feature of Psalms poetry, see Patrick D. Miller Jr., "The Theological Significance of Biblical Poetry," in *Language, Theology, and the Bible: Essays in Honour of James Barr*, ed. Samuel E. Balentine and John Barton (Oxford: Clarendon, 1994), 213–30.

6. Allen P. Ross, *A Commentary on the Psalms*, Kregel Exegetical Library (Grand Rapids: Kregel Academic, 2013), 2:365. The Hebrew word is *'ak*.

7. The Hebrew word *nepeš* has various meanings, from neck to life, from breath to soul. For further study, see my "Direct Reflexivity in Biblical Hebrew: A Note on נפש [*nepeš*]," *ZAW* 129 (2017): 411–26.

8. On the Hebrew lexemes for silence, see the detailed study by Sanja Noll, *The Semantics of Silence in Biblical Hebrew*, Studies in Semitic Languages and Linguistics 100 (Leiden: Brill, 2020).

stretch of simply not speaking? Perhaps it is an inner calm or a gritting of the teeth without using words. In any case, these questions
are not answered—not yet, anyway. Opacity builds tension, and thus
the prod of poetry is felt. But before moving on, the psalmist gives
us a sense of direction. It is *to* (or *for*) God that his soul is in silence,
and it is *from* God that the psalmist has salvation.[9] The poet's world
is defined by God, by God alone. The confidence in silence comes
from knowing the direction of deliverance.[10]

Images are piled on the hearer: God alone is the rock, salvation, and
fortress. The psalmist breathes relief. Whether heavy rain or enemies
come, God is there, a certain safety. The psalm continues but directs
its words to the attackers. Quite unimpressed with them, the psalmist
asks, "How long" will they go on with such foolish acts (v. 3)? This
question cuts both ways. Certainly, it is *for the persecutors*, but since
the psalm is a prayer, this implies that the question is also *for God*.
Similar to Psalm 13, the basic inquiry is "How long, . . . O Lord[?]"
(62:1, 11).

Metaphorical language highlights the idiocy of the antagonists.
Knocking down a leaning wall needs little skill or strength. There
is an implicit mocking of the would-be strong: they are merely bul-
lying the already bruised. While this may be physical, it is certainly
verbal (v. 4). They give praise and kindness with their lips, but when
it is advantageous, they slander. Here is a reminder of how the world
works. These fools are groping in the dark; thankfully, the psalmist
reminds us of the light.

Verses 5–6 repeat earlier phrases and bring the poem home. Silence
is before God "alone."[11] The repetition of this line, however, has
variation, a feature that is typically significant in reading Scripture.[12]
Verse 5 does not state what the psalmist is doing (cf. v. 1) but rather
what he should do: "Be silent!" The precise meaning of the silence

9. These are *'el-'elōhîm* and *mimmenû yeshûatî*, respectively.
· 10. Cf. Ross, *Commentary on the Psalms*, 2:367.
11. Translating *'ak lē'lōhîm*.
12. See recent study of parallelism: Robert Holmstedt, "Hebrew Poetry and the
Appositive Style: Parallelism, *Requiescat in pace*," *Vetus Testamentum* 69 (2019): 617–
48; cf. Michael O'Connor, *Hebrew Verse Structure* (Winona Lake, IN: Eisenbrauns,
1980). For a nuanced and careful articulation of parallelism in Hebrew poetry, see
F. W. Dobbs-Allsopp, *On Biblical Poetry* (New York: Oxford University Press, 2015).

evades scholars: the verb is ambiguous. Worse still, some translations, such as the NRSVue, state it as an action, "My soul *waits*," instead of an imperative, "Be silent, O my soul." Some think the silence is a call for a calm disposition; others think of it as not speaking, all while still being anxious.[13] There is no easy answer. The pressure of poetry is leveraged, and we must wait to feel the full force of the poem.

It becomes apparent why the psalmist can (or should) be silent: his hope is *from God*. The psalmist is crying out at a time when his hope has not been realized. There is a patience, a not-yet-ness. The difference between defining God by circumstances, as is so often done, and defining circumstances in light of God is slowly becoming apparent. Psalm 62 is another reminder that life is not cinematic, with easy problems and quick solutions—answers taking no more than two hours to achieve. A list of steps or a practice of rituals will not suffice either. Equally deficient is life as curated on social media. This is a pressured life, a life that, as verse 5 claims, is not smooth. Hope rests in God, in "God alone."[14]

Verse 8 brings us to the corporate scene and makes certain that we all have something to learn. We are greeted by simplicity and clarity: "Trust in him at all times." *Trust* is an inner state with outward evidence, and it's a favorite word in the Psalms.[15] Notably in our psalm, "Trust is the attitude the psalm has expressed (vv. 1–3a) and has urged on the self (vv. 3b–7), *without using the word* [until v. 8]."[16] Where we see trust, we see the absence of shame. Where we find trust, we find confidence. Trust and deliverance go hand in hand. A steady life, albeit filled with difficulties, knows that God is true, real, strong, listening, and ever protective.

In a season of struggle, Psalm 62 offers challenge and encouragement. This trust is not simplistic or mechanistic, as if one can simply trust and then quickly all things will go right. It is, on the contrary, something real and worthy. The call to trust in the pressured moments of life presses us to consider life more carefully. While it may seem

13. For the latter position, see Goldingay, *Psalms*, 2:248.
14. Cf. Hossfeld and Zenger, *Psalms 2*, 115.
15. As in Pss. 21, 28, 37, 84, 112 (v. 7), 115, 135.
16. Goldingay, *Psalms*, 2:249 (emphasis added). The explicit call to "trust" is from the psalmist to his audience (vv. 8, 10).

trite or elementary to "trust God" in the throes of life, other options prove disappointing. From others to ourselves, from technology to retreats, nothing can sustain the weathered soul like God himself. This is not to dismiss the role of the community but to make it clear that God *alone* is the one in whom we trust: there is no other. Our confident refuge is in God.

We should pour out our hearts before God (v. 8). The imagery here is key.[17] Pouring out, like oil or a cup of water, implies giving all of it. So what resides in our heart, not simply emotions but also our thoughts and those things deep within—that is what we pour out. But note to whom: it is "before him [God]" that we do so.[18] In life, we need not look the part of having it all together, but merely be ready and willing to pour it all out. God is our "refuge."

Our next two verses (vv. 9–10) remind us why God—and *only* God—is worthy of our trust, of our confidence, of pouring out our hearts. Here we recognize the human condition. Humanity is frail and quickly gone. We are bent toward delusion. Put us on a scale, and we do not weigh it down. The picture here shows the madness of it all. If humanity is a quick and deluded people, why put your trust in them or anything they do? It must be said that this is no support of nihilism or pessimism, but a signpost for where we can find the one who is our refuge.

We are reminded not to find safety or security in money or in the crooked ways people go about getting it. Even if money increases, our trust is not in it. From this, the psalmist pivots to speak directly to God. The poem ends with the recognition that strength and loyal love are with him. As the poet struggles through the pressures of life, he knows that above all, in the weakness of humanity, there is strength in God. When we are utterly unreliable, God's love is sure and steady, committed to himself and directed outward to humanity. We come to this truth by way of ambiguity within poetry as we slowly read

17. For an enlightening look at metaphors in Psalms, see Pierre van Hecke and Antje Labahn, eds., *Metaphors in the Psalms* (Leuven: Peeters, 2010); the exceptionally clear monograph by Alison Ruth Gray, *Psalm 18 in Words and Pictures: A Reading through Metaphor*, BI 127 (Leiden: Brill, 2014); and the influential book by William P. Brown, *Seeing the Psalms: A Theology of Metaphor* (Louisville: Westminster John Knox, 2002).

18. In Hebrew, *ləpānāyw*, "before him [God]," v. 8.

how the psalmist communes with God in dark times. Throughout the psalm, we experience ambiguity, but that draws us closer to the poetry and asks us to listen ever more closely to its music. The psalm welcomes us to the reality that God is strong and his love is firm: he is our refuge. This poem shapes our soul in such a way that our confidence is put in no one else.[19]

19. Allan Ross puts it well: "This psalm is a beautiful display of confidence in the LORD." *Commentary on the Psalms*, 2:375.

— 11 —

Turns in Poetry

PSALM 73

What's the point of it all? Why go through the pain and the precision of maintaining integrity when people who flaunt evil flourish? These aren't easy questions. Thankfully, they're not particularly novel questions either. In Psalm 73, the psalmist grapples with righteousness, the wicked, and the purpose of life. "This psalm is one of the 'peak texts'" of the Old Testament, as it speaks to the pervasive difficulties of a life of faith.[1] Nevertheless, it is poetry, and so much remains tacit.[2] The poem "records the inner journey of one who has come within a hair's breadth of abandoning hope in the justice

---

1. Frank Lothar Hossfeld and Erich Zenger, *Psalms 2: A Commentary on Psalms 51–100*, trans. Linda M. Maloney, Hermeneia (Minneapolis: Fortress, 2005), 238.
2. In terms of its form, the psalm is especially difficult to categorize, as scholars well note. See, e.g., Catherine Petrany, "Words Fail Me: Silence, Wisdom, and Liturgy in Psalm 73," *JTI* 13 (2019): 114; Jacqueline E. Lapsley, "'Bring On Your Wrecking Ball': Psalm 73 and Public Witness," *Theology Today* 70 (2013): 63; Walter Brueggemann, *From Whom No Secrets Are Hid: Introducing the Psalms*, ed. Brent A. Strawn (Louisville: Westminster John Knox, 2014), 127.

of God."[3] This journey presents us with one of the most dramatic poetic turns in all the Psalter. The poet builds to this turn by way of other features we've looked at previously: repetition, paradox, and juxtaposition. In the psalm, we have opportunity to ponder faith by listening in on a saint who is carefully considering life and all its vicissitudes.

The first line sets the stage. God's goodness is declared in the first verse, and in the closing verse the psalmist affirms this goodness. The structure propels us through the poem—first talking *about* God (vv. 1–17), then talking *to* God (vv. 18–28)—all with emotionally charged language wrestling with a world that appears anything but right.[4]

——————————— **PSALM 73** ———————————

A Psalm of Asaph.

[1] Surely God is good to Israel,
    to those who are pure in heart.
[2] But as for me, my feet had almost stumbled;
    my steps had nearly slipped.
[3] For I was jealous of fools;
    I continually saw the peace of the wicked.

[4] For they have no pain in their death;
    their bodies are sound and sleek.
[5] They are not in trouble as others are;
    they are not plagued like other people.
[6] Therefore, arrogance is their necklace;
    they wrap themselves in violence.
[7] Their eyes bulge from fatness;
    the imagination of their heart has no limit.
[8] They scoff and speak with malice;
    loftily they threaten oppression.
[9] They set their mouths against heaven,
    and their tongues range over the earth.

3. J. Gordon McConville, *Being Human in God's World: An Old Testament Theology of Humanity* (Grand Rapids: Baker Academic, 2016), 199.
4. Hossfeld and Zenger, *Psalms 2*, 224.

¹⁰ Therefore, the people turn and praise them,
and find no fault in them.
¹¹ And they say, "How can God know?
Is there knowledge in the Most High?"
¹² Such are the wicked;
always at ease, they increase in riches.
¹³ Surely in vain I have purified my heart
and washed my hands in innocence.
¹⁴ For all day long I have been plagued
and am rebuked in the mornings.

¹⁵ If I had said, "I will talk on in this way,"
I would have rebelled against a generation of your sons.
¹⁶ But as I considered to know this,
it was toil in my eyes,
¹⁷ till I went to the sanctuary of God;
then I discerned their end.
¹⁸ Surely you set them in slippery places;
you cast them to ruin.
¹⁹ How they come to destruction in but a moment,
swept away utterly by terrors!
²⁰ They are like a dream when one awakes;
on awaking, you despise their phantoms.

²¹ When my heart was embittered
and my kidneys pierced,
²² I was but a fool and did not know;
I was like a beast with you.
²³ Nevertheless, I am continually with you;
you grab my right hand.
²⁴ You guide me with your counsel,
and afterward you will receive me with honor.
²⁵ Whom have I in heaven but you?
And there is nothing on earth that I desire other than you.
²⁶ My flesh and my heart may fail,
but God is the rock of my heart and my portion forever.

²⁷ Indeed, those who are far from you will perish;
you put an end to those who are false to you.
²⁸ But for me, it is good to be near God;
I have made the Lord GOD my refuge,
to tell of all your works.

The poem begins with a theological reflection. "Surely God is good to Israel" (v. 1).[5] This regionalized note makes sense within the context of the Hebrew Bible. The juxtaposition within the line, however, is not to be missed; God stands in relation to goodness. What's more, the poet stresses this fact with "surely" (*'ak*).[6] The poem now unfolds. We read that God's goodness "is . . . to those who are pure in heart" (v. 1). Perhaps this is referencing the faithful *within* Israel, or the line may extend *beyond* the bounds of Israel.[7] In any case, this theological backdrop of God's goodness exacerbates the psalmist's experience. The psalmist's "feet had almost stumbled; / [his] steps had nearly slipped" (v. 2). The relationship of goodness and the psalmist remains to be explored—so we press on.[8]

The psalmist's near fall comes from being "jealous of fools" (v. 3). By piling the lines one on another, the psalmist intimates that the jealousy was due to "the peace of the wicked," which he continually saw (v. 3). This line exhibits the paradox of Scripture's poetry. How is it that the wicked have peace? This should not be the case; nonetheless, the psalmist is observing that reality is out of shape.[9] This tension should be felt as we read.

The poem specifies the absurd thriving of the wicked. For instance, "they have no pain in their death; / their bodies are sound and sleek" (v. 4).[10] Their bodies testify to pampered care and accoutrements;

5. For an insightful and accessible discussion of theology of God and his goodness, see Christopher R. J. Holmes, *The Lord Is Good: Seeking the God of the Psalter*, Studies in Christian Doctrine and Scripture (Downers Grove, IL: IVP Academic, 2018).

6. Notably, Augustine Marie Reisenauer discerns structure in the psalm based on the repetition of "surely" / "indeed": vv. 1–12 (*problem*); vv. 13–17 (*transition*); vv. 18–28 (*resolution*). See "The Goodness of God in Psalm 73," *Antonianum* 86 (2011): 16–17.

7. The first possibility would mean a more specific group within the nation of Israel, whereas the line could well be saying the "pure in heart" is an explanatory gloss on all of Israel.

8. It is possible that a rather technical, though highly artistic, literary structure is at play—namely, the "ring composition": vv. 2–3; vv. 4–12; vv. 13–17; cf. Hossfeld and Zenger, *Psalms 2*, 221–38.

9. The *yiqtol* form seems to have some explanatory power here. The psalmist appears to be reflecting on not only what has happened in the past but also on what he is currently experiencing.

10. This is an especially challenging verse textually, but clarity resounds in that the wicked are enjoying life. Note that, textually, the phrase "in their death" is question-

what's more, they are not "in trouble" or stricken as are other humans
(v. 5). The lines imagine these people shuffling through life unscathed.
As Walter Brueggemann puts it, "Their bodies are healthy and reek of
self-care."[11] As irritating as that image might be, the true vexation is
that these people, who are "bursting with health, . . . carefree[,] and
have a lust for life," are called "fools" and "wicked" (v. 3).[12]
    We recall that we live in a moment of distraction and amusement
(cf. chap. 1 above). The phrase "self-care" is leveraged by modern
marketers to sell the latest pampering products. We hope we can
instantly click our way into a life of health, convenience, and most
importantly happiness. The present moment welcomes the wicked
to publicly and proudly display a life edited down to only pleasure.
For those with faith in the living God, this is a tenuous time. The
seemingly pain-free life of the wicked parades about. The context of
the psalmist's problem may be all too similar for us today.
    These nameless fools wear their confidence for all to see. The next
lines, filled with clothing metaphors, demonstrate the disposition and
action of the wicked ones. "Therefore, arrogance is their necklace; /
they wrap themselves in violence" (v. 6). Their agency speaks to their
character and gives detail to theological complexity. Some people
actively engage in folly; why should they flourish? The following lines
incite more questions rather than offer answers.
    The "eyes" and "heart" of the wicked invite the reader to consider
life's desires. Frustratingly, these fools' "eyes bulge from fatness; /
the imagination of their heart has no limit" (v. 7). The people are
seemingly unchecked and unbridled: the wicked do as they please.
The remainder of this section details their derisive speech. "They
scoff and speak with malice," out of arrogance (v. 8); "they set their
mouths against heaven, / and their tongues range over the earth"
(v. 9). Clothing, speech, and unrestrained cravings flatten zeal for
following God. This senseless flourishing prods the psalmist (and
reader) to ask, What is the point of it all?

able. Interestingly, Walter Brueggemann and William H. Bellinger render the clause
"For they have no pain." *Psalms*, New Cambridge Bible Commentary (New York:
Cambridge University Press, 2014), 316.
    11. Brueggemann, *From Whom No Secrets Are Hid*, 128.
    12. Hossfeld and Zenger, *Psalms 2*, 228.

The speech of fools gets more specific as well as more theological. "They say, 'How can God know? / Is there knowledge in
the Most High?'" (v. 11). With deep displeasure, the psalmist re-
ports, "The wicked [are] always at ease" and "increase in riches"
(v. 12). Reality crumbles the psalmist, and the poetry now reckons
with this. The psalmist admits, "Surely in vain I have purified my
heart / and washed my hands in innocence" (v. 13). The logic is
plain and painful that the former efforts in holiness were a waste.
What is more, the psalmist, in contrast to the wicked, has been
struck "all day long . . . / and . . . rebuked in the mornings" (v. 14).
Things are not as they should be. The wicked prance about uncon-
strained while the psalmist has been carefully attending to his life and
innocence.

The thick tension of faith waits for some release within the poem.
Recall that the Lord "is good to Israel, / to those who are pure in
heart," and that the psalmist "had almost stumbled" (vv. 1–2). Resolution remains unspoken, at least for now, as the self-diagnosis of the
psalmist has done no good; clarity is not within reach.[13]

The psalmist underscores the dejection rampant in the world. If
he had declared all this, he "would have rebelled against a generation
of [God's] sons" (v. 15). Nothing but turmoil would have awaited
such expounding by the psalmist. The poet presses on in the fog of
life: "As I considered to know this, / it was toil in my eyes" (v. 16).
Reflection does not satisfy the psalmist; that tension, the outlook of
no hope, sets the stage for one of the most significant theological
turns in the book of Psalms.

To prepare for this turn, we need to recognize that within verses
15–16, the psalmist refuses to speak. This observation can cut several
ways. Catherine Petrany asks, "Is this the silence that the psalms
so often associate with misery, lifelessness, and death, or does the
psalmist's verbal restraint here carry some positive communicative
value within the context of the psalm as a whole?"[14] We wait for an
answer. As we do, we recognize that "the protagonist of Psalm 73
stops speaking altogether, and does this *prior to* an encounter with

13. Hossfeld and Zenger, *Psalms 2*, 225.
14. Petrany, "Words Fail Me," 117.

God."[15] Vexingly, though, this silent "reflection and brooding (v. 16a) only sharpen the crisis."[16]

Verse 17 pivots the psalm and the faith of the psalmist, who struggles *until* he goes to "the sanctuary of God." Nothing is given about the process or the activities, only the *place*.[17] In this space, the psalmist discerns the wicked's end in "a kind of retrospective silence."[18] Crucially, Gordon McConville observes that the "change in the psalmist is not brought about by material alternations in external reality, but entirely inwardly, in a transformed perspective on the nature of things."[19] In "a moment of religious focus, everything veers sharply in a new direction."[20] The haze of wicked living and well-being now clears. The psalmist (recall chap. 1 above) is not distracted or bored in either the situational or the existential sense. Attention is squarely on the living God.

On the other side of the sanctuary, the psalmist speaks directly *to* his God, in contrast to speaking *about* him. Verse 18 stresses the Lord's agency in bringing an end to the wicked: "Surely you set them in slippery places; / you cast them to ruin." These lines ring in the ear. The poem begins with the psalmist nearly falling (v. 2). The psalm also opens with "surely ['ak]," thus emphasizing God's goodness. Much of the early part of the poem struggles to reconcile the goodness of God and the psalmist's crisis. Yet upon being in the presence of the Lord (v. 17), the psalmist understands that the wicked will indeed slip and fall. Importantly, the wicked do so not as happenstance, but at the will of the Lord. Reflection enables the psalmist to see rightly: "How they come to destruction in but a moment, / swept away utterly by terrors!" (v. 19).

The psalmist reviews his previous pain: "When my heart was embittered / and my kidneys pierced" (v. 21).[21] The next verse reads, "I

15. Petrany, "Words Fail Me," 121 (emphasis original).
16. Hossfeld and Zenger, *Psalms 2*, 230.
17. See further Carolin Neuber, "Space in Psalm 73 and a New Perspective for the Understanding of Ps. 73:17," *Biblical Interpretation* 29 (2020): 279–307.
18. Petrany, "Words Fail Me," 124.
19. McConville, *Being Human*, 199.
20. Brueggemann, *From Whom No Secrets Are Hid*, 129.
21. In the ancient world, "heart" and "kidneys" were used to connote both emotion and decision-making (Jer. 11:20; 12:2; 20:12).

was but a fool and did not know; / I was like a beast with you" (v. 22). The first line of verse 22 describes by way of category; the psalmist was "a fool." The second line evocatively tells what the psalmist was like. Stupidity burdened the poet, and the reader is meant to feel that weight as the psalmist describes himself as "a beast."

The poetry moves forward, yet it repeats the language from verse 22. Verse 23 begins with "Nevertheless, I . . ." as a way to signal some relationship to the previous lines. The poet contrasts the past from his present and states that he is "continually with you [the LORD]" (v. 23). This line at least hints that the presence of the Lord is beneficial to the psalmist, rather than punitive.

Once again, divine agency is stressed: "You [the LORD] grab my right hand" (v. 23). The poem refuses some notion of pure human independence. The living God would seem to reach out and hold the psalmist's hand as a parent would a child's. In that vein, the poetry emphasizes the counsel by which the Lord leads the psalmist (v. 24).

Recalling for all who would listen, the psalmist states the singularity of the Lord's power and provision.[22] The two lines of verse 25 combine to show that neither heaven nor earth has anything or anyone that can help—except the Lord. Verse 26 begins to draw the experience of the psalmist to a close: "My flesh and my heart may fail, / but God is the rock of my heart and my portion forever." The anatomical imagery highlights the frailty of humanity. This reality, however, is only an introduction to the theological truth that the Lord is the psalmist's strength. In this poetic moment, we glimpse the beauty of humble, confident weakness. The poetry wrestles with fragility and dependence: weakness is certainly not a problem, as long as it is tethered. God is the portion of the psalmist, and this truth teaches, corrects, and soothes the soul.

The final two verses of the poem return to the topic of wicked and righteous, but they do so with spatial descriptions (vv. 27–28). The poet draws attention with the word translated as "indeed" or "look." What follows is about "those who are far from you" (the Lord). Their future reality, much unlike the first half of the poem, is

---

22. I infer "provision" in part from the use of *ḥelqî*, "my portion" (cf. Pss. 119:57; 142:5; Lam. 3:24).

destruction. They, as with the path of the wicked in Psalm 1, "will perish" (1:6; 73:27). The psalmist declares, "You [the LORD] put an end to those who are false to you." This verse, aside from setting the wicked in proper view, provides the immediate contrast for the poet in the following lines.

Verse 28 draws together "good" and "God" in a way that reminds readers of verse 1 yet significantly differs from it.[23] The psalm begins by asserting God's goodness for Israel and the pure of heart (v. 1). This truth lays the groundwork for the psalmist's spiraling faith, since his surroundings and confession do not match—until the psalmist comes "to the sanctuary" (v. 17). Everything changes, and the poem then concludes, "But for me, it is good to be near God" (v. 28). What's more, the psalmist declares, "I have made the Lord GOD my refuge" (v. 28). For the poet, the Lord is a proximate safety; yet if the reader is left unphased by these lines, then they have not, at least in a true sense, read the poem. God's good and protective nearness demonstrates that the flourishing of the wicked is fleeting. The ephemeral pampered life of fools has no real power to deconstruct the psalmist's faith.

As we pick up these pages of Scripture, we do so not merely to inspect an interesting literary artifact, but to have our souls shaped. Through the tightly compact lines of poetry, the repetition of what is "good," the comparison of those "near" God with those "far" from God, and the paradox of the faithless flourishing over and above the faithful—all such features instruct us, mind, body, and soul. These features center around the great turn that happens in the sanctuary. Through the poetry, even in the hardest of days, the Holy Spirit teaches our hearts to hear the fullness of the truth: God's presence brings clarity and protection for those pure of heart (vv. 1, 28). What's more, wickedness will not win out. The final line, "to tell of all your works," reveals that "the psalmist can and does speak."[24] The silence is lifted: praise to the living God abounds.[25] The psalm concludes in "personal testimony and . . . proclamation."[26] May it be so with our lives as well.

23. Reisenauer, "Goodness of God," 11.
24. Petrany, "Words Fail Me," 126.
25. Petrany, "Words Fail Me," 126.
26. Hossfeld and Zenger, *Psalms 2*, 236.

– 12 –

Worship in Poetry

PSALM 96

To many readers today, Israel, the nations, and the natural world seem to be distinct, unrelated topics. This may especially be so because the Old Testament focuses on the story of *Israel*. Such a generalization by moderns holds truth and untruth. Certainly, Israel is front and center throughout the Hebrew Bible, yet attention on the nations, aside from them merely being a thorn in the side of Israel (cf. 1 Samuel), runs all through Scripture. The poetry of Psalms easily draws together these "others" as fellow choir members who sing a chorus to the one and only God. Nevertheless, the most striking, if not bewildering, intersection comes with the introduction of the *natural world*. Here we are challenged head-on to consider (or reconsider) our view of nature. Psalms poetry, which nourishes our life as a "praying existence," stretches our theological imagination in this poem.[1] Accordingly, we are instructed in what the worship of

1. Hermann Spieckermann, "From the Psalter Back to the Psalms: Observations and Suggestions," *ZAW* 132 (2020): 18.

the Lord looks like. If we have a vision of the world that counts all things physical as evil, meaningless, or both, then we might quickly skip over an entire section of Psalm 96. Yet this poetry has the power to hold our attention and awaken our imagination to the world in which the seas, the skies, and all in between praise the Lord alongside Israel and the nations.

PSALM 96

¹ O sing to the LORD a new song;
   sing to the LORD, all the earth!
² Sing to the LORD, bless his name;
   tell of his salvation from day to day.
³ Declare his glory among the nations,
   his wonders among all the peoples!
⁴ For great is the LORD and greatly to be praised;
   he is to be feared above all gods.
⁵ For all the gods of the peoples are vain,
   but the LORD made the heavens.
⁶ Honor and glory are before him;
   strength and beauty are in his sanctuary.

⁷ Ascribe to the LORD, O families of the peoples,
   ascribe to the LORD glory and strength!
⁸ Ascribe to the LORD the glory due his name;
   bring an offering, and come into his courts!
⁹ Worship the LORD in the splendor of holiness;
   writhe before him, all the earth!

¹⁰ Say among the nations, "The LORD reigns!
   Yes, the world is established; it will not shake;
   he will judge the peoples in uprightness."

¹¹ Let the heavens be glad, and let the earth rejoice;
   let the sea roar and all that fills it;
¹² let the field exult and everything in it!
   Then shall all the trees of the forest sing for joy
¹³ before the LORD, for he comes,
   for he comes to judge the earth.
He will judge the world in righteousness
   and the peoples in his faithfulness.

The first line of the psalm pauses the reader. The opening call is "Sing to the LORD a new song!" The request is repeated, "Sing to the LORD," with a vocative that might well be evocative. Put differently, to what or whom is "all the earth" referring? The simple phrase sparks the mind. Is this meant as the natural land? The word "earth" easily connotes the physical land apart from anything that resides in or on it (say animals and humans).[2] In addition, it could well mean the physical land *including* the living creatures within it and things on it.[3] What's more, the phrase could certainly connote humans. In providing the interpretive options, the purpose is not to burden the reader, but to offer up what the poetry in fact provokes. In any case, we see a strong and clear call to sing that incorporates voices *outside of* Israel.

Every line adds specificity to the poem. As we read, the psalm is inviting us to sing along. Those who follow the living God are given constant instruction and detail on what singing should sound like. For instance, verse 2 repeats "Sing to the LORD" but adds "bless his name." Both calls are clear but general. The second line of verse 2 brings precision: "Tell of his salvation from day to day." This declaration is meant to highlight salvation, which can have at least two different referents. One, the historical deliverance of Israel from the Egyptians could be recalled and sung. Two, the salvation professed could well be what the hearers themselves have experienced. A definitive reading isn't possible. This salvation is, nonetheless, generalized such that it elicits our own experience with the living God. We as readers are drawn in and called to sing out the salvation of God. In reading just the first two verses, our souls are shaped and our mouths are opened to praise the Lord.

Verse 3 adds texture to the scope and content of the singing. "Declare his glory among the nations" reads the first line, and this provides some tension. We have seen that the call is for "all the earth" to sing, but with verse 3 the directionality pivots so that these singers perform their song "among" or "in" the nations. Is Israel alone meant to be the singer here? Conceivably, it's the faithful *within and among*

2. Gen. 18:2; Exod. 23:10.
3. Cf. 1 Sam. 14:25; 27:9; 2 Sam. 15:23.

the nations who are prominent. The second line of this verse brings more intensity: "[Declare] his wonders among all the peoples." The content of their singing is thus "the wonders" of God. This word conjures up the amazing deeds that the Lord has done to and against the Egyptians (Exod. 4–14). Certainly, the Lord exhibited his glory and wonders in the exodus, and those historical realities could be the primary, if not the exclusive, referent in mind. I suggest, however, that the lines of poetry piled up with "all the earth" (v. 1) bring awareness to the readers' thought that God's "glory" and "wonders" have also been experienced by us as well. Therefore, as we rehearse this psalm, we do so not only recalling the exodus but also recognizing God's *wonders* in this world today.

The call to sing is grounded in theology. The bodily praise is not sourced from emotion or mere circumstance, but from God himself.[4] In other words, declare his glory, "for great is the LORD" (v. 4)! In quick succession, the poem reminds the reader that "the LORD [is] greatly to be praised" and "to be feared above all gods" (v. 4)! The psalm points to the truth that the Lord is worthy of praise far above any other deity. Theological honesty underwrites the people's collective singing; with this realization, the poetry has opportunity to scaffold the soul. The Scriptures begin to work on us. These realities that undergird praise are not conditioned on specific events, past or present; rather, these reasons are direct affirmations of who the Lord is.

The following verse reiterates the worthiness of God. The first reason for praise comes in comparison: "All the gods of the peoples are vain" (v. 5). The worthlessness of these gods points to the wonder of the Lord, as cited in the preceding lines. The second line of verse 5, seemingly a non sequitur, states abruptly that "the LORD made the heavens." The quick turn from vain gods to the Creator God negates the virility of these handmade gods and, in succinct fashion, highlights the power of the Lord. These rather straightforward lines of poetry more than hint that a proper view of creation—being, indeed, the work of God the Creator—speaks deeply to the physical, verbal praise of the Lord. The reader is, therefore, encouraged to praise.

---

4. See further W. David O. Taylor, *A Body of Praise: Understanding the Role of Our Physical Bodies in Worship* (Grand Rapids: Baker Academic, 2023).

Verse 6 seems to follow the reasoning above. Staccato lines lead with similar yet distinct notes of honor, glory, strength, and beauty. In some form or fashion, all four come wrapped up in the presence of the divine. The first two, "honor and glory," are before God. The second pair, "strength and beauty," are said to be "in his sanctuary." Thus, to be in the presence of the Lord is to be amid his honor, glory, strength, and beauty. Of all these, the second pair is the most intriguing because these words are only occasionally juxtaposed. In all, the worship of the living God speaks to the reality of honor, glory, strength, and beauty in his presence.

In a cultural moment when both strength and beauty are contorted, misunderstood, and misappropriated, a poetic vision proves insightful. Thus, we shouldn't look to ads, social influencers, and political machines to gather a sense of beauty and strength. Rather, these are in some way related to the presence of God since they are "in his sanctuary" (v. 6).

We return to the call. Commands fill nearly every line of the next four verses (vv. 7–10). As with previous lines loaded with imperatives, we move from the most general to the most specific action. For instance, the ones called to "ascribe to the LORD" are in fact the "families of the peoples" (v. 7; cf. Gen. 12:3). The second line tells of the content: "Ascribe to the LORD glory and strength." This line could fit nicely in nearly any psalm, yet it finds particular resonance here because of the stipulation that "strength" as well as "glory" and "honor" are predicated upon the Lord's presence (v. 6). In other words, the listener should sing back to God who he is. Similarly, the following line (v. 8) tells all to "ascribe to the LORD the glory due his name." Once again, we hear echoes from before. Earlier, the poem called all to "bless his name" (v. 2), then later to "declare his glory" (v. 3). All this ascribing is reified in the second line of verse 8: "Bring an offering, and come into his courts." These majestic and lofty calls for worship are physically embodied in the offering.

A physical posture of praise leads the next two verses (vv. 9–10). Recall that we are reading poetry and not a to-do list; thus, this psalm doesn't serve as a mere instruction manual. It is, nonetheless, instructive for theology and practice. The first line of verse 9 is the most straightforward: "Worship the LORD in the splendor of

holiness." Embodied humility flows from this line, and the following
line opens new vistas: "Writhe before him, all the earth" (v. 9). Once
again, we are squaring off with the problem of reading poetry. What
exactly is meant by "all the earth"? The first line of the psalm brings
symmetry to the present verse but does not uncomplicate the matter.
The scope of writhing is wide.

In verse 10, we meet another call for the listeners to speak something in and "among the nations" (cf. v. 3). The first line unfolds
theology in a way that the reader of the psalm has not yet experienced. They should "say among the nations, 'The LORD reigns!'"
This one phrase grounds the earlier poetry that puts "strength and
beauty" near the Lord and declares that "honor and glory" are due
him (vv. 6, 8). The reach of "all the earth" praising the Lord (v. 9)
has something to do with the fact that "the LORD reigns!" (v. 10).
Since we are reading a poem, we do not receive a lecture in full about
how all this works. Nonetheless, we are tutored, through the quick
layering of lines, that the praise to the Lord and the rule of the Lord
go hand in hand.

The following lines draw out various implications of the fact that
the Lord reigns. For instance, "The world is established; it will not
shake" (v. 10). The world moves along as it should because the Lord
is King. Such a recognition prompts further questions: If the Lord
reigns, then how can this or that happen? We begin to fill in the
blanks and prod around the question. Often, we are only seeking to
see whether such a note matches our lived experience. The poetry
does not answer all our inquiries but stimulates further reflection,
and I suggest that's by design. With each poetic line, we gain clarity
and have more to consider. Our rumination does not stop when the
poem is finished. This verse concludes with notes of justice (vv. 10,
13). While another line on reigning is unsurprising given the start of
verse 10, the scope and manner of the Lord's kingship bring precision. The Lord "will judge *the peoples in uprightness.*" Both Israel
and the nations will receive God's judgment. Our hearts should be
encouraged by this truth.

The final section of the poem stands in stark contrast to what many
moderns may think. In what might seem out of place, the psalmist
invites the natural world to praise. The volume is loud and the choir

large. Verse 11 incorporates "the heavens," "the earth," "the sea," and
"all that fills it." Song fills the air with verbs like "rejoice," "roar," and
"exult." Verse 12 highlights "the field exult[ing]" and "all the trees
of the forest sing[ing] for joy." The booming chorus is performed
"before the LORD" (v. 13). These created components of the natural
order join together in praise and, in so doing, give us pause to take it
all in.

Too easily can we skip over the concluding section of the psalm. We
might too quickly label these moments as metaphorical or anthropo-
morphic. Such categories would in large part miss the freight of the
poetry. In these concluding verses, we hear and feel the summons to
praise. Nations, peoples, all the earth, fields, trees, and water usher
forth joy and praise before the Lord. The poetry has no qualms about
hearing humans and nature sing side by side. Recognizing this, we
catch a better glimpse of creation at large. All who are beckoned in
this psalm are creatures: a fundamental feature of creaturehood is
praise to the Creator God. Dependency is built into the fabric that
God has sewn; reliance takes shape in different ways throughout the
book of Psalms, be it lament, thanksgiving, or praise. In Psalm 96,
creaturely dependence on the Lord stirs the congregation to sing.

The relationship of the Lord to creation receives more notice in
the final lines of verse 13. The Lord "comes to judge the earth." This
line reinforces the earlier declaration: "He will judge the peoples in
uprightness" (v. 10). Different and indeed more evocative is the fact
that, according to verse 13, the Lord is about "to judge the earth."
This seems to include not just peoples and certainly not just Israel.
The entirety of creation—fields, forests, and more—will be judged.
The following lines bring specificity in that the Lord "will judge the
world in righteousness / and the peoples in his faithfulness" (v. 13).
There is no place or thing outside the scope of the Lord's reign.

As earlier in the psalm, the final section of the poem challenges
our view of nature and our view of ourselves. The poetry instructs
our prayers and praise by forming our theological imagination of
worship and the world. If we look at the natural world as meaningless or purely instrumental for our own sake or profit, then we
misunderstand. That is, the heavens, the sea, and the trees are not
simply for the ever-increasing economy, nor are they meant merely

for admiration. They praise! What's more, these lines confront our supposed human autonomy; human beings are set to receive the judgment of the living God, the one who "made the heavens" (v. 5) and reigns as King (v. 10). This sobering poetry also brightens the heart since judgment is to be rendered in "uprightness," "righteousness," and "faithfulness" (vv. 10, 13). The world and all that is in it will be made right. In light of that reality, Psalm 96 calls the whole earth to sing a new song.

– 13 –

Creation in Poetry

PSALM 104

God is great. This true statement resonates in many situations. He is great and "above all gods" (Ps. 135:5). He is great in that his love abounds (145:8). The portrait of Holy Scripture offers many scenes of God's greatness (Deut. 7:21), and the poetry of Psalms sketches out specific features of his majesty. In Psalm 104, the greatness of God intersects with creation and praise, and does so through concise and compact lines filled with metaphor. This psalm "is arguably the greatest hymn to the glory of creation in the Hebrew Bible."[1] At a distance, the psalm reads like Genesis 1–2: both writings reflect on the created order.[2] Mountains, land, light, darkness, and more overlap

---

1. Robert Alter, "The Glory of Creation in Psalm 104," in *Biblical Poetry and the Art of Close Reading*, ed. J. Blake Couey and Elaine T. James (New York: Cambridge University Press, 2018), 51. Additionally, see Benjamin Abotchie Ntreh, "The Survival of Earth: An African Reading of Psalm 104," in *The Earth Story in the Psalms and the Prophets*, ed. Norman C. Habel (Sheffield: Sheffield Academic, 2001), 98–108.

2. In fact, Ps. 104, being "the most extended explication of God's work of creation outside of Genesis, . . . deserves a central place in any attempt to think about God as creator and about the doctrine of creation." Patrick D. Miller Jr., "The Poetry of

in these two texts. Nevertheless, the purpose of the poetry here differs from that of the Bible's earlier chapters. The works of the Lord prompt the psalmist to bless, sing, and make melody (vv. 1, 33).

In this poem, our soul is shaped by rehearsing the created works of God. Perhaps to the chagrin of some, reading the poem does not primarily result in working out the relationship of science to Scripture; instead, hearing the theological details of the created order provokes us to praise. God's character, wisdom, and power in ordering creation are on display in this poem, and crucially, these are not merely facts to understand.[3] Instead, our intellect and imagination are captured by the strong beauty of God's care; on account of such benevolence, we sing. In short, the images and terse lines in Psalm 104 make "us aware how much *poetry is the proper language of creation*," in that "God's act [of creation] . . . is complex and beautiful."[4]

─────────── **PSALM 104** ───────────

[1] Bless the LORD, O my soul.
    O LORD, my God, you are very great.
You are clothed with honor and majesty,
    [2] wrapped in light as with a garment.
You stretch out the heavens like a tent;
    [3] you set the bars of your chambers in the waters;
you make the clouds your chariot;
        you ride on the wings of the wind;
[4] you make the winds your messengers,
        fire and flame your ministers.

[5] You set the earth on its foundations,
        so that it shall never be shaken.
[6] You cover it with the deep as with a garment;
        the waters stood above the mountains.
[7] At your thunderous rebuke, they flee;
        at the sound of your thunder, they scurry.

Creation: Psalm 104," in *God Who Creates: Essays in Honor of W. Sibley Towner*, ed. William P. Brown and S. Dean McBride Jr. (Grand Rapids: Eerdmans, 2000), 87.
    3. I thank Sarah Haynes for her wisdom here.
    4. Miller, "Poetry of Creation," 96 (emphasis original).

⁸ They rose up to the mountains, ran down to the valleys,
   to the place that you appointed for them.
⁹ You set a boundary that they may not pass,
   so that they might not again cover the earth.

¹⁰ You make springs gush forth in the valleys;
   they flow between the hills,
¹¹ giving drink to every wild animal;
   the wild asses quench their thirst.
¹² By the streams, the birds of the air have their habitation;
   they sing among the branches.
¹³ From your lofty abode, you water the mountains;
   the earth is satisfied with the fruit of his work.

¹⁴ You cause the grass to grow for the cattle
   and plants for people to use,
to bring forth food from the earth
   ¹⁵ and wine to gladden the human heart,
oil to make the face shine
   and bread to strengthen the human heart.

¹⁶ The trees of the LORD are watered abundantly,
   the cedars of Lebanon that he planted.
¹⁷ In them, the birds build their nests;
   the stork has its home in the fir trees.
¹⁸ The high mountains are for the wild goats;
   the rocks are a refuge for the rabbits.

¹⁹ You have made the moon to mark the seasons;
   the sun knows its time for setting.
²⁰ You make darkness, and it is night
   when all the animals of the forest come creeping out.
²¹ The young lions roar for their prey,
   seeking their food from God.
²² When the sun rises, they withdraw
   and lie down in their dens.
²³ People go out to their work
   and to their labor until the evening.

²⁴ O LORD, how many are your works!
   In wisdom, you have made them all;
   the earth is full of your creatures.

[25] Yonder is the sea, great and wide;
     creeping things innumerable are there,
     living things both small and great.
[26] There go the ships
     and Leviathan, which you formed to sport in it.

[27] These all look to you
     to give them their food in due season;
[28] when you give to them, they gather it up;
     when you open your hand, they are filled with good
         things.
[29] When you hide your face, they are dismayed;
     when you take away their breath, they die
     and return to their dust.
[30] When you send forth your spirit, they are created;
     and you renew the face of the ground.

[31] May the glory of the LORD endure forever;
     may the LORD rejoice in his works—
[32] who looks on the earth and it trembles,
     who touches the mountains and they smoke.
[33] I will sing to the LORD as long as I live;
     I will sing praise to my God while I have being.
[34] May my meditation be pleasing to him,
     for I rejoice in the LORD.
[35] Let sinners be consumed from the earth,
     and let the wicked be no more.
     Bless the LORD, O my soul.
     Praise the LORD!

In the opening verse, the poem calls for the psalmist (and in turn the reader) to "bless the LORD." The reason follows in the next line, but it does so without any formal marking, not even with "for" or "because." The psalmist speaks directly to God: "O LORD, my God, you are very great" (v. 1)! The poetry allows for this line to underwrite the opening call to worship, while still leaving much unsaid. We may well ask, Why is the Lord so great? The remainder of the poem goes a long way in answering that question.

Imagery floods the following verses (vv. 1–4), and clothing metaphors frame a number of lines. The Lord, for instance, is "*clothed* with honor and majesty, / *wrapped* in light as with a garment" (vv. 1–2). God wears light and splendor as we do a shirt, and his radiance is something he himself puts on. Indeed, "the description is amazing."[5] With these lines, we experience what was said over a century ago about the psalmist: "*This poet is a master of form and of expression.*"[6] The rest of verses 2–4 stresses God's acts and abode within creation. He stretches out "the heavens like a tent" and sets "the bars of [his] chamber in the waters" (vv. 2–3). Clouds are his chariot, and the wind is the road where he rides (v. 3). Furthermore, the winds and flame of fire are his works and ministers (v. 4).

This initial section (vv. 1–4) of the psalm stirs the imagination. We are in awe of the sky not simply for its beauty, but because God figures creation as his instrument. The majesty vision of the Lord riding clouds like a chariot and the flame of fire as apprentice moves the mind to consider God's greatness afresh.[7] We are awakened to the fact that the world—its sky, water, clouds, and wind—is the Lord's work.

In the next section, the poem reflects God's ordering of the land, sea, mountains, and valleys (vv. 5–9). A fundamental feature of the Lord's having established land is that it "shall never be shaken" (v. 5). When God sets the earth "on its foundations," nothing can displace his arrangement. This simple reflection has significant reverberations. These two lines demonstrate that the Lord's power and authority are unmatched. Land, then, is not merely evidence of some intelligent design, but instead an indication of the power of the living God. This reality can grip us in our everyday, mundane activities, whether eating toast in the morning or driving to work. When headlines or harried paces of life dominate our hearts, we can be set aright and readied to praise by this poetry. This is not self-talk to improve our mood,

---

5. Konrad Schaefer, *Psalms*, Berit Olam (Collegeville, MN: Liturgical Press, 2001), 257.

6. Kemper Fullerton, "The Feeling for Form in Psalm 104," *Journal of Biblical Literature* 40 (1921): 45 (emphasis original).

7. This is not the place for detailed deliberation on the role of human dominion within creation (cf. Gen. 1–2) or the challenges of creation care today. For a good resource on this topic, see, e.g., Douglas J. Moo and Jonathan A. Moo, *Creation Care: A Biblical Theology of the Natural World*, Biblical Theology for Life (Grand Rapids: Zondervan, 2018).

but reckoning with the theological reality of creation: this Creator God has not been dethroned; he is King and Creator.

God's relation to the waters cannot be missed here (v. 7). His "thunderous rebuke" causes the waters to "flee" and "scurry." Creation moves at the sound of the Lord's voice. Not only that, mountains and valleys go exactly to the place that the Lord has "appointed for them" (v. 8). Where God makes "a boundary," no water will "pass" or "cover the earth" (v. 9). Thus, as we look around at the earth's topography, we begin to see the Lord's order, his borders, and the result of his voice (vv. 5–9).

Far from superfluous, the movement of water results in the nourishing of wildlife. The living creatures and "wild asses" are watered and "quench their thirst" (v. 11). Birds find rest and raise their voices (sing) over the water and in trees (v. 12). In short, it is by "the fruit of the [Lord's] works" that "the earth is satisfied" (v. 13). The poetry proves that our imagination of creation should include not only the Lord's power and creation rightly ordered, but also the earth's satiation.

The following section highlights the materiality and blessing of harvest (vv. 14–23). Beasts and human beings receive crop and grass because the Lord causes things to grow (v. 14). Production results in food of all sorts. For instance, "wine to gladden the human heart, / oil to make the face shine, / and bread to strengthen the human heart" (v. 15). Beyond people, the trees, mountains, hills, and rocks serve birds, goats, and rabbits (vv. 16–18).[8] Each area of creation noted in the poem is fitted for serving another part of creation. God's design is stunning: "The harmony between humankind and the animal kingdom is firmly stressed."[9] Yet that realization should not leave us as admirers only, but rather put us into the posture of worshiping the living God.

The moon and sun find prominence in verses 19–20. The psalmist leverages these lights to clarify how creatures within God's order thrive. For instance, it is in the "night" that "all the animals of the

---

8. Robert Alter's translation of v. 16 is particularly striking: "The trees of the Lord drink their fill." Alter, "Glory of Creation," 50.

9. Alter, "Glory of Creation," 52.

forest come creeping out" (v. 20). Creation's dependence on the Lord is a salient feature of this poem. Notably, "lions" are "seeking their food *from God*" (v. 21). Lions "lie down" when the sun rises, whereas people "labor until the evening" (vv. 22–23). The sequence of light and darkness provides order to life. According to the psalm, these creaturely comings and goings are not simply awaiting scientific explanation (though they may welcome such); the patterns give witness to the Lord's power to order and preserve.

The poem pauses, and the psalmist reflects: "O Lord, how many are your works!" (v. 24). Patrick Miller finds that the "whole point of the psalm is expressed" in this line.[10] The stress, however, is not only in the innumerability of the Lord's works; it's that the Lord "in wisdom, . . . made them all" (v. 24). Creation is witness to God's wisdom. Our thoughts, songs, prayers, and poems must reckon with this reality. The truth of creation's design cannot be told without reference to the Lord's wisdom. The poem centers our attention and shapes our soul to the theological reality of the world that is around, above, and under us. Seas and creatures are countless and due to God's forming them (vv. 25–26).[11]

Creation's reliance on the Lord can hardly be overstated. Line after line, Holy Scripture instructs our mind on the way the world works (vv. 27–30). "All" creatures wait for the Lord "to give them their food in due season" (v. 27). No matter who works or hunts, provision comes from the Lord. As God gives, "they gather it up" (v. 28).[12] As God opens his hand, "they are filled with good things" (v. 28). With these lines, we recall that "the earth is satisfied with the fruit of [the Lord's] work" (cf. v. 13). This reality is formed by the Lord kindly choosing to "open [his] hand" (v. 28).

The darker side of God's greatness finds reference as well. If the Lord hides his face, then creatures "are dismayed" (v. 29). When he

10. Miller, "Poetry of Creation," 92.

11. Alter observes that though Leviathan appears in the psalm, it is "in almost comically reduced dimensions" ("Glory of Creation," 52). The sea creature is neither a real nor perceived threat to the Creator God. Alter even states that Leviathan "is turned into God's aquatic pet" ("Glory of Creation," 57). Similarly, J. Clinton McCann Jr. says this "mythic sea monster . . . has become God's beach toy." McCann, "Between Text and Sermon: Psalm 104," *Interpretation* 66 (2012): 69.

12. The constant use of "when," preceding the subject "you [Lord]," colors the entirety of vv. 28–30.

"take[s] away their breath, they die and return to their dust" (v. 29). Life and death rest in the Lord's hand (cf. 1 Sam. 2:6). No hint of pure human autonomy can be found in the psalm. Whatever creatures do, they do it while depending on the Lord, as the following verse emphasizes (v. 30). When the Lord sends his spirit, creatures are created and he renews the land (v. 30). Life, its inception and endurance, is sourced in the Spirit of God.[13]

It is reasonable to move from reflection on creation to praise. This psalm does that very thing, but not in the mode expected. The psalmist calls for "the glory of the LORD" to last forever (v. 31); the following line in the verse surprises: "May the LORD rejoice in his works." This vision of the Creator rejoicing over his creation provides a corrective to any model that views the Lord as detached and unconcerned. Joy reverberates through the Lord's reflection on his own works. Our soul is shaped so that joy and song intersect when considering the works of the Lord.

The power of the Lord gives opportunity for astonishment. This poem "is a splendid piece of poetry, marshaling radiant imagery to express the speaker's sense of the glories of God's creation."[14] The poem tells us that the Lord "looks on the earth and it trembles" (v. 32). He "touches the mountains and they smoke" (v. 32). This truly awesome power prompts song and melody by the psalmist (v. 33). The psalmist will "rejoice" not merely in creation but also "in the LORD" (v. 34). Our eyes are directed not primarily to the created order, but to God himself. The marvelous, powerful, and wise acts of the Lord order creation and, in turn, nurture our hearts. Praise flows forth.

Similar to Psalm 1, this psalm does not conclude on a note of happiness. There is the call, seemingly out of nowhere, for "sinners" to be wiped away "from the earth" and "the wicked [to] be no more" (v. 35).[15] Yet as Miller aptly states, "one who has read the Psalter from the beginning should not be surprised that a reference is made to the

---

13. For further discussion, see the recent book by Jack Levison, *A Boundless God: The Spirit according to the Old Testament* (Grand Rapids: Baker Academic, 2020).

14. Alter, "Glory of Creation," 59.

15. I find Alter to be quite off the mark here as he renders the lines about sinners and the wicked (v. 35) as "no more than a small oddity before the conclusion." Alter, "Glory of Creation," 60.

sinners and the wicked."[16] Once again, we are reminded of the two unambiguous paths in Psalms: life and death. There is no gray area to explore. For as open and ambiguous as psalms poetry is, the paths of the wicked and righteous are clearly separate. In Psalm 104, the psalmist does not seem to entertain some admixture of righteous and wicked; it is one or the other. The modern reader who wants to savor the supposed space between the righteous and wicked is sure to be disappointed. The poem, with all its notes of dependency and praise, sobers us to the reality of wickedness. Despite the gravity of death, the psalm ends the way it began, with blessing and praise (vv. 1, 35). Accordingly, the poem, through tightly packed lines filled with metaphor, instructs that we are to be instruments that bring songs of praise to the Creator God. In a way that no other literature can approximate, this poetry intertwines creation and praise so that instruction and joy animate the reader. Blessed be our God!

16. Miller, "Poetry of Creation," 94.

– 14 –

The End of Poetry

PSALM 150

New Orleans is the place I call home. This historic city is known for many things, from jazz to crawfish, but it's perhaps most famous for Mardi Gras. People come from around the world to take in the unparalleled atmosphere and tradition. Some people can imagine Mardi Gras only as a debauched celebration of the most depraved aspects of humanity; though carrying a ring of truth, such a conception is only a caricature. Should you come to the Crescent City for this long-awaited season, you'd experience a myriad of sounds and sights that welcome families. You'd see young children sitting atop ladders with signs; you'd notice men and women—who on other occasions are quite reserved—jumping, yelling, waving, and dancing, all on the prospect of catching some beads tossed from decorative floats. You'd find loud, joy-filled, community-embracing crowds embodying one thing above all else: celebration.

Psalm 150 reminds me of Mardi Gras. Both are unapologetically loud. My guess is that readers unimpressed with Psalm 150 are like the same people you can find at Mardi Gras sitting in a lawn chair, off at a distance, complaining about being there. Some of us (I'm including myself here) feel more comfortable muting the final psalm of the Psalter rather than listening to the music as written. This short poem, teeming with repetition, trains us in the nature and purpose of praise.

─────────────── **PSALM 150** ───────────────

¹ Praise the LORD!
Praise God in his sanctuary;
    praise him in his mighty heavens!
² Praise him for his mighty deeds;
    praise him according to his surpassing greatness!

³ Praise him with trumpet sound;
    praise him with lute and harp!
⁴ Praise him with tambourine and dance;
    praise him with strings and pipe!
⁵ Praise him with sounding cymbals;
    praise him with loud clashing cymbals!

⁶ Let everything that has breath praise the LORD!
    Praise the LORD!

"Psalm 150 shows us how to make an end of things."[1] This short poem has three parts, each answering a question. "Why?" is handled in verses 1–2; "How?" in verses 3–5; "Who?" in verse 6.[2] Symmetry is found in nearly every line, beginning with the call to "praise" (*halălû*). This praise is expressly directed to the Lord (vv. 1, 6). Nine times, the command rings out, "Praise him." Verse 6 exhibits a significant distinction: it's the only line in the entire poem that does not begin with an imperative of praise, but instead the line starts, intriguingly and explosively, with "*Let everything*." Before reaching the final line, let's read through the short poem and let each line build anticipation.

1. Jason Byassee, *Psalms 101–150*, Brazos Theological Commentary on the Bible (Grand Rapids: Brazos, 2018), 248.
2. This structure is noted by Friederike Neumann, *Schriftgelehrte Hymnen: Gestalt, Theologie und Intention der Psalmen 145 und 146–150*, BZAW 491 (Berlin: de Gruyter, 2016), 393, 395.

Verse 1 stresses praise in places: "*in* his sanctuary" and "*in* his mighty heavens."[3] Verse 2 lays the predicate for praise, "his mighty deeds" and "surpassing greatness."[4] As noted throughout the book, praising the Lord has virtually nothing to do with present experience. Put differently, the psalms don't entertain the question of how to get into the mood to praise. In our moments of distraction, boredom, and curiosity, the last psalm puts praise as the last word. The motivation rests on who God is, recognizing "his mighty deeds" and "his surpassing greatness" (v. 2).

The next section of the poem outlines the instrumentation (vv. 3–5). We begin to hear the music as the instruments are gathered: "trumpet," "lute and harp," "tambourine and dance," "strings and pipe," and "cymbals." We don't need to dive into the history books to see how instruments in ancient Israel were different from those today. The congregation is summoned to praise and to do so with musical instruments. Given the clarity and simplicity of words throughout Psalm 150, *understanding* is not difficult, nor is it the end of interpretation. The psalm means to move hearts. In this psalm, we see no docile, underwhelming setting, but loud praise of the living God. The volume may be welcomed by some or rejected by others. But it can't be missed that *this* psalm is the poem that ends the book—not Psalm 1, with its wisdom on flourishing; or Psalm 23, with its confidence in the great shepherd; or Psalm 3, with its cries to the Lord.[5] The finale of praise teaches us something about the shape of faith. Our eyes are lifted above the fray to the greatness of the Lord God. The response from the soul shaped by the book of Psalms is as simple as it is significant: *praise*. This doesn't minimize our difficulties or pain (see above, esp. chaps. 6, 8, and 11), but it does aim our attention right. Praise bursts forth in the final verse of the poem.

Verse 6 begins with "let everything." How fitting! The last verse of the Psalter is not meant for a Davidic king or Israel exclusively.

---

3. On the "heavens" in Ps. 150, see the connection to Ps. 19. Neumann, *Schriftgelehrte Hymnen*, 398.

4. Neumann reads the "greatness" here with the predicate of "the LORD" as King in Pss. 95:3 and 145. *Schriftgelehrte Hymnen*, 401.

5. The Psalter is not a haphazard collection; as I argue in chap. 2, it's not a narrative either.

Worship of the living God is a worldwide event. The constant call to avoid idolatry (e.g., Exod. 20) seems to show that worship is a natural human activity. Throughout the book of Psalms, worship is encouraged and shaped; Psalm 150 puts a fine point on it. In this short verse, "everything that has breath" is urged twice to "praise the LORD." Words, music, and dancing as expressions of worship are due to only one: the holy God.

All this truth within the psalm moves us to worship. Indeed, "by praising the greatness of the Lord, his worshipers implicitly acknowledge their own creaturely dependence on him."[6] We should certainly recognize that "it is the privilege and obligation of mortals, as they worship the Lord, to join the mighty chorus that the morning stars began, and Psalm 150 invites all people everywhere to do that."[7]

We live in an age of distraction, as chapter 1 outlines. For pilgrims who have traveled with Psalm 150 and sung the psalm, rehearsing the poem once again may seem boring. We may well want some spectacle, something novel.[8] We could look around, with hubris so readily accessible, and find nothing in Psalm 150 that electrifies us, nothing overly enthralling. Yet the poetry has the ability to focus our attention, and in doing so, awaken us to praise.

The Psalter ends with praise. Put differently, the Psalter does *not* end with us. The telos is fully revealed in that the poetry—through all its images, short lines, openness, repetition, paradox, emotions, and more—takes our words where they belong, to the one and only God. The loud praise poem has the ability to drown out the distractions of this age, but our heart needs to be habituated by the Holy Spirit. The poetic Scripture called Psalms deserves our attention. Through its sweetness, we can practice what it is to pray, praise, worship, and adore the Lord God.

6. Daniel J. Estes, *Psalms 73–150*, NAC (Nashville: B&H, 2019), 634.
7. Estes, *Psalms 73–150*, 638.
8. I thank Sarah Haynes for her insights here.

Afterword

Silent and Solitary

In the sectors of evangelical Christianity that I know, it is common to hear the admonition "Read your Bible." From an early age, I was instructed to carve out a time in the morning to open my Bible, read for a few minutes, and pray. This was known as "quiet time" or "time with the Lord." A key feature would be a silent, solitary reading from the Bible. For some people, partly based on how they were taught, this quiet time has become definitional for their faith. For instance, if someone has "missed a few days," they could feel as though their faith is weakening or growing cold.

This view of Bible reading shapes nearly every student I teach in seminary. They are also helped along by other professors who challenge them to do this very thing and, at times, caution them if they have not been doing so daily. My own journey through theological education proved the same. One of my own professors taught plainly that my health as a Christian and especially a pastor is fundamentally based on this time with the Lord. I've heard pastors, teachers, and speakers introduced with accolades for their reputation of keeping their quiet time. They're consistent in this spiritual discipline, and so they're commended, perhaps above any other discipline or virtue.

I'm a child of this teaching. I doubt I would have become a Bible major in college, earned a PhD in Old Testament, or traveled the

147

world to read, write, and present research on Holy Scripture if this specific view of the Bible were not humming along in the back of my mind. I've learned many lessons from the steady challenge to go home and read the Bible. It's natural to pick up the Bible and read, being prepared to be taught through correction, rebuke, and encouragement. I don't by any means want to dismiss the significant benefits of this culture of Bible reading. Nevertheless, there is at least one unfortunate and significant (though unintended) consequence of this pervasive view of faith.

The most obvious example is seen in my students. For graduate students, many of whom are preparing for some type of ministry, I teach courses on the Old Testament and biblical Hebrew. No matter the specific course, students read numerous Old Testament texts. A curious thing happens, usually around midterms. Students look out of sorts and often vocalize how out of balance they feel. "I'm doing all this assigned reading from the Bible, but I'm not having my quiet time," they say. They feel guilty and ashamed. Their schedules are pushed to the limit. Some work one or two part-time jobs, have a full load of graduate hours, are reasonably social, are involved at their local church, and as mentioned in the opening chapter of this book, are deeply committed to "vegging out," "bingeing," and "unwinding" with various kinds of digital media. Needless to say, their morning hours for quiet time are taken up with sleep or study (typically the former, based on my observation). They're *not* doing what they've been taught for the last twenty years or so in church, and they feel miserable.

One way to address such students—or others working full-time with significant responsibilities or the ever-busy stay-at-home moms or dads—is to discuss the details of time management. Break out the quadrants of urgent, nonurgent, important, and unimportant. I've heard sages in the church and seminary go this route. I'm sure I've done the same too. Certainly, we all could tighten up our use of time, right?

I recall students who (unprompted) disclosed to me that they've maxed out their schedule; there's no way they can be any more efficient in their studies, they tell me. In effect, they want to earn an A in my course, but they are likely on a path to score a B or a C. I have been moderately sympathetic to such students, knowing some of their responsibilities. Before long, these students were confessing their uninterrupted clutch on their phone and their preoccupation with social media. Whatever the individual case, we can all stand to do a little better in making use of the time we have.

Time management, however, is not where I direct students to go these days. Instead, I'm focused on bringing the theology of Holy Scripture to my students and any others for whom I'm responsible, be it my family, the local church, or my readers. First, the Bible is living, active, holy, and pure. There is no spatial constraint for the efficacy of Scripture. That is, we do not get a sense that the Bible is *more* holy or *more* active if it is read in specific spaces; this is especially so with regard to homes. Nowhere, for instance, does the Bible seem to catechize an exclusively early morning session of Bible reading by individuals in the home. In fact, the instructions of God seem to be democratized in terms of time. In the great text of Deuteronomy, we imagine learning, reciting, and teaching the words of God in the normal paces and places of life. Second, Holy Scripture is for hope. It is not designed as a manual giving "a word of encouragement for the day." A morning pick-me-up to feel a bit better about the day is far from Scripture's purpose. Reading Psalms could well provide this kind of sugary inspiration, but only at the real expense of avoiding the struggle and pain so pervasive in the poetry throughout the book.

There is a third aspect that is not regarded often enough. The running assumption throughout Scripture is *not* that readers silently and individually scan the Bible in the comfort and privacy of their homes. The gathered community of saints is the normalized (though *not* exclusive) setting for Holy Scripture. Two rather obvious and inter-related things need mentioning here. Scripture is meant to be *heard* by the community; Scripture is intended to be *read aloud*. The history of the church shows these two points to be reified in the reading of Psalms in worship. Certainly, there is historical precedent for silent, meditative reading by individuals; indeed, I'm not suggesting that we abandon reading the Bible silently and solitarily in our homes. What I am saying, however, is this: *Scripture should be read aloud often and at length to the gathered body of Christ.*

The Psalms Together

To get a glimpse of how Scripture can be the language of the church today, I'd like to tell how my local congregation, Immanuel Community Church in New Orleans, recites and reads the Holy Bible.[1] I don't highlight the church as *the* example or illustrate from a condescending disposition. I merely offer the church as an embodied example of engaging with Scripture, a church that has dramatically shaped my life and my family. Immanuel is a faithful congregation, and much thought has been given to how and why Scripture is read in weekly gatherings.[2] Below are some standard features of our corporate gatherings.

Our service begins with the pastor welcoming everyone and then reading a psalm that calls us to worship. Following that, we sing two songs together. Next, as a congregation, we recite a different psalm. Over the course of this year, these have been Psalms 1, 13, and 23. We stay with one psalm recitation for three months. At the moment of writing, we are working on Psalm 16. Part of the intent is that we memorize these psalms. Recitation is reinforced in our home groups that meet during the week. As each midweek gathering incorporates the scheduled psalm, and the aim of this practice is that our souls will be shaped by the words of Psalms, to prepare us to lament and praise, as well as everything in between.

Outside of Psalms recitation, fairly early in the Sunday gathering, one member of the congregation will stand and give a reading from the Old Testament and one from the New Testament. These readings are typically quite long. Each consists of nearly one chapter. Following that, we have a pastoral prayer and then one more corporate song. Once our pastor comes to the preaching event, he will, as a matter of course, read the passage to be preached. He is currently preaching through the book of 1 Samuel. Thus, in a normal gathering of Immanuel on Sundays, this amounts to hearing two psalms, two additional readings (Old and New Testament), and the text for

---

1. See also Brent A. Strawn, *The Old Testament Is Dying: A Diagnosis and Recommended Treatment*, Theological Explorations for the Church Catholic (Grand Rapids: Baker Academic, 2017), 213–42.

2. I should add that this was the case well before I arrived.

the sermon. For the uninitiated, this may seem daunting, boring, and excessive.[3] A few comments should help show why those initial impressions don't win out.

First, it is a deeply theological position that Holy Scripture is meant to be *effective* in the life of the church. Notably, this hearing is in several instances unadorned. That is, for the two psalms and the Old and New Testament readings, no commentary, exhortation, illustration, or application is added. Second, it is good for us to hear the Bible read aloud together as the gathered church. While it is wholly appropriate to read Scripture alone and silently each morning in our houses and apartments, that is no substitution, our church believes, for hearing the words of God *together*. Third, our congregation (myself included) can grow in our skills of listening and our ability to focus our attention. Perhaps the best way to do so is through continued practice. Thus, we rehearse this habit every week.

This experience with sisters and brothers in Christ has become one of the sweetest, most enriching, and most expectant moments in my weekly rhythm. There have been days when I'm tired, distracted, or both. Some readings and recitations are boring (most likely on my account as a hearer). I've also listened through a reader fumbling their words or putting the wrong emphasis in the reading. But I've learned that this is altogether okay. I return the next Sunday, prepared to hear Scripture again.

This rhythmed life has been a fairly drastic shift for me. I've been in churches where only a few verses have been read at a given gathering. During one season, lasting about three years, the primary exhortation of the sermon week after week was "Go home and read your Bible." Again, as a professor of Old Testament, I could (at some level) get behind the admonition. Yet it was clear that nearly every scriptural text for the sermon had at its center something *other* than getting people to disperse and read the Bible alone. I knew there was a better vision of preaching. What's more, somewhere deep down in my bones, I understood that there was a better, richer, more thoughtful, and indeed more theological way for the church to engage the

---

3. In other traditions, of course, this is quite normal.

Scriptures. Immanuel has been the embodiment of healthy practice, for which I'm deeply grateful.[4]

Nevertheless, the vision of faith being synonymous with personal morning Bible reading remains strong. One Sunday, while traveling, my family and I visited a lovely church. We were welcomed and encouraged to sing praises to God. In the sermon, a young preacher was walking line by line through Colossians 2. The text is a rich, deeply christological passage that speaks of the wonder of baptism and faith as well as the challenges of surrounding philosophies that are empty and vain. In Colossians 2:7, the preacher encountered key clauses, such as "rooted and built up in him," but could not offer up the treasures of the verse except by glossing the theologically rich phrases as synonymous with personal quiet time. From there, the young man confessed his unsteady habit of reading Scripture in solitude. Some weeks were good; some weeks were bad. Nonetheless, he encouraged himself and the congregation to press on and keep at it. As he was riffing on his application, my wife—who, as far as I know, is the gentlest, kindest, most encouraging woman that has ever lived—leaned over and quietly said, "I don't think the apostle Paul has a morning quiet time in mind when he writes about being rooted in Christ." My wife is almost never wrong.

All this is to say, we need to be reminded—fairly often, I think—that Scripture shapes our heart and mind. It is especially significant to hear Psalms and the rest of the Bible read and recited in the corporate gatherings of the saints. As we're a distracted people, let's constantly renew our attention to the potent poetry of Psalms. Through such work, may the Holy Spirit teach and admonish us, to the glory of God the Father, in the name of the Son. Amen.

---

4. I should add here recognition of the sweet times spent at and with Eden Baptist in Cambridge, England, over the years. This congregation opened my mind and ears to better practices with respect to the corporate reading of Scripture.

Scripture Index

153

Author Index

Thomas Aquinas, 9, 15, 15n57
Torrance, Thomas F., 22n3

van der Merwe, Christo H. J., 72n3
van Harn, Roger, 5n6
van Hecke, Pierre, 112n17
Villareal, Erin, 45n18

Wallace, David Foster, 5, 5n8
Wallace, Robert E., 25n15
Waltke, Bruce K., 57n18, 78n3
Webster, John, 14, 14nn45–48, 14nn50–52,
    15, 15nn53–61, 16,s 16nn62–65, 17nn66–
    69, 17nn71–72, 56n12
Weeks, Stuart, 52n3

Weil, Simone, 11
Willgren, David, 22n7
Williams, Joshua, 24n13
Wilson, G. H., 21n1
Wirzba, Norman, 71n2
Wittman, Tyler R., 39n11, 40nn12–13
Wright, N. T., 5n7, 95n11

Yarchin, William, 25n17

Zenger, Erich, 36n4, 108n4, 111n14, 115n1,
    116n4, 118n8, 119n12, 120n13, 121n16,
    123n26
Ziegert, Carsten, 96n14

Subject Index

metaphor in, 39
prayer in, 10n33
as Scripture, 34
thirsting in, 102
openness
and curiosity, 12
of language, 26, 28, 35–38, 49, 63, 75–81,
103, 146
overstimulation, 7

paradox, 18, 26, 39–42, 49, 84, 86, 91–98,
116, 118, 123, 146
and God, 91
and Jesus Christ, 40, 86
and pain, 92
parallelism, 31, 110n12
patience, 71, 94, 111
and metaphor, 38, 99–100

qatal, 80n4, 96n12

repetition, 83–89, 92–93, 105, 116, 123, 144,
146
and ambiguity, 107
and boredom, 83
and memory, 61, 68
with variation, 110
rest, 78. See also sleep
ring composition, 118n8

self-care, 8, 119
shame, 16, 98
absence of, 111
and theology, 42
silence, 40, 108–111, 120–21, 123
and lexemes for, 109n8
and solitude, 13
and study, 13
terror of, 5
sleep
and boredom, 79
business of, 79
lack of, 52
and theology, 78
solitude, 152
and silence, 13
and study, 13
spectacle, 13, 26, 146

Spirit of God. See Holy Spirit
Stevenson, Robert Louis, 7
story
of Israel, 125
Psalms as, 18, 21, 23–25, 25n5, 28–29, 31,
32n44
See also metanarrative
study, 13, 14
and boredom, 13
and curiosity, 12
and desire, 15
and focal practice, 9, 14
of God, 15
and habit, 16
and silence and solitude, 13
spirit of, 10
symmetry, 43, 72, 130, 84, 144
lack of, 69
syntactical connection. See logical connector

technology, 7, 11, 61, 112
critique of, 4n5
as distraction, 7, 8, 11
and Holy Spirit, 17
telos, 7, 71
and praise, 146
theology, 42, 44, 57n18
of attention, 5, 8–18
and creation, 86, 138
of dominion of God, 89
of flourishing, 67
of goodness of God, 118n5
of Holy Scripture, 149
and imagination, 44
and lament, 52–54, 79, 94
and praise, 128
and prayer, 17, 30
and Psalms, 21, 30, 53n5, 84n6, 129
and shame, 42
and sleep, 78
and speech of enemies, 77
Thomas Aquinas, 9, 15
time management, 148–49

vengeance, 35–36
vindication, 37

yiqtol, 78n3, 96n12, 118n9